My Life Story Part Two

My Professional Life

First Published in Great Britain 2024 by Mirador Publishing

Copyright © 2024 by Chris Hawley

All rights reserved. No part of this publication may be reproduced or transmitted, in any form or by any means, without permission of the publishers or author. Excepting brief quotes used in reviews.

First edition: 2024

A copy of this work is available through the British Library.

ISBN: 978-1-915953-91-9

Mirador Publishing
7 Cossington Lane
Woolavington
Somerset
TA7 8HL

My Life Story Part Two

My Professional Life

Chris Hawley

Dedication

This book is dedicated to my two Daughters, Isabel and Cathy and my Son, Christopher, who were all a delight to bring up.

Working in England

Forest Hill

MY SCHOOL HAD NO CAREERS guidance mechanism, and consequently, I had no clue about what to do on leaving school. I took History and Geography at 'A' level and passed in both. They were my favourite subjects. I have always had a vivid imagination, and the pages of History came alive for me. I could see the historical characters as if they were with me. Novels set against a historical background have always been a favourite source of reading. Geography, particularly the branch dealing with our physical world, has never lost its fascination. Like many people, I used to doodle a lot. My favourite doodle was to draw shapes around words on a page, until the lines brought the shapes together. The end result would look like a relief map of islands, with mountains and valleys. Once space exploration became a reality, I was, and still am, moved by the view of our world from space; the colours, the oceans, the mountains and the deserts. Judging by these early inclinations, I might have made a career in cartography or archeology.

My creative talents were late in showing themselves. At eighteen years old I was still a child. I could blame the British education system for not bringing out latent skills in me, but again, it may just have been my nature. I am sure I was not alone. And think how important this is; to find the career best suited to the school leaver! How much better contribution would be made to the development of society, if the young person is in the career he or she is most comfortable in! I have often thought in later life that I would have been happy as an architect. At eighteen, I didn't know what I wanted to do, so I allowed my father to choose for me. He chose a career with his best intentions for my future happiness, and I pursued that career for thirty years. It was in my hobbies and activities outside office hours that I developed my other talents and passions, and found an outlet for my creativity. It is not that I have been unhappy in the career he chose for me. In fact, it suited my character in some ways. The opening in the Accountancy profession came about this way.

Dad had worked in Kuwait since 1954. The auditors of the Kuwait Oil Company were a firm of Chartered Accountants based in the City of London. Thomson McLintock & Co. was a major Scottish firm, with offices in Edinburgh, Glasgow and London. At the end of the audit of the Company's books, one of the partners of the firm visited Kuwait. This is a normal procedure for large companies. Mr. C. R. Smith met my father at a social gathering during the partner's short visit. Dad mentioned that I was leaving school, and what was the possibility of my pursuing a career in Accountancy. Out of that talk came an interview, and finally I became articled to Mr. Smith for a period of five years. That is how I eventually became a Scottish Chartered Accountant. I began my apprenticeship on the 19th September 1960.

It was Dad's home leave from Kuwait that year. A memorable holiday was spent in our beloved Devon, staying in The Moorlands Hotel, Lydford, and during which we enjoyed our special stream and surrounding moorland, as well as days spent motoring around Devon and Cornwall in a hired Ford Zodiac. It was also the holiday during which Dad bought the 18.56 acres of land on the road to Hatherleigh. Once Dad had returned to Kuwait, the rest of the family dashed back to Devon for another few days, before returning to Green Harbour, our bungalow in Upper Basildon. Unfortunately, no photographs of that holiday survive.

During those few days between Mum's sad task of settling John and Jean in their respective schools on the 14th and 15th and my first day at work on the 19th, she and I spent a quiet weekend, birdwatching in the woods around Upper Basildon. We had already been shopping for my office attire. I remember clearly the grey overcoat and green felt trilby that I wore to work that autumn, but especially the waistcoat; green on one side and a brown check on the other. I loved that waistcoat, and it kept me warm during many winters. Gloves, umbrella, neck-scarf, briefcase, dark suit and tie and black shoes completed the outfit that stamped me as a City worker. It was fashionable at that time to wear a bowler hat and a long, dark overcoat, but I thought it too sombre, and actually it was already going out of fashion. A rolled-up newspaper added a scholarly touch to the figure, provided it was a respectable daily! Train journeys to the office were mostly silent, with many minds trying to unravel the cryptic clues of the crossword. Starched white collars could still be seen and looked spectacular against a colourful striped shirt. I often saw a rose pinned to the left lapel of a suit jacket and coloured handkerchiefs were often worn in the top pocket. Many older men would still be wearing gold pocket watches, but they were no longer in fashion. Of women's fashion I recall little, but I suspect the older ladies were still wearing the fifties dress; conservative and unprovocative. The miniskirt was yet to shock the world!

During the first week at work, Mum and I must have stayed with her parents in Riefield Road, Eltham. Her diary provides no information, but tells of another important event in my life. It was on that Friday that Mrs. Reeve came into my life. It was fixed on the spot: I was to board there at four guineas a week from Sunday the 25th September. I vividly remember a photo of me with Mr and Mrs Reeve, taken in their back garden on that day; the photo now sadly lost. Having sorted out the wardrobe, Mum and I retreated to Upper Basildon for the weekend. On the following Saturday, we drove back to London early to Jean's school in Chislehurst, to take her out for the day. On the following day, we got up at 5 am and drove down to Wantage to have a last few hours with John. Mum flew back to Kuwait on the 4th October, having successfully performed her duties, while I settled in at Mrs. Reeve's house.

No. 7, St. German's Road was to be my home for the next three years. The semi-detached house was built with typical London yellow brick, three stories high, with a front and back garden and a side entrance, but no garage, the house having been built before cars became part of our lives. The street led off the Brockley High Road, close to the junction with the main road between Forest Hill and Catford. As the crow flies, I think it cannot have been more than two miles from where I was brought up. The nearest railway station was Forest Hill. The underground did not serve that particular suburb of London.

Mrs. Reeve was a little, round, grey-haired woman about sixty years old. She had no children of her own, but gave her love to the boys she looked after, cooked for, washed clothes for and mothered. She was much more of a mother to me than a landlady! She went to the extent of cooking a roast dinner with roast potatoes every day of the week for us; not just a roast, but roast beef with Yorkshire pudding and horseradish sauce, or roast pork with apple sauce, or roast lamb with mint sauce, or roast chicken with bread sauce. I would come home from work to find the dear lady standing over the kitchen stove, with a fag hanging from her lips, red in the face, preparing a delicious meal that her boys would always appreciate. Her roast dinners were never to be forgotten! One of us would enter the kitchen and pull her apron strings; perhaps more than one of us! She would always pretend to be cross, and chase us out of the kitchen with a wooden spoon, or with whatever she happened to be holding. But she loved the attention. She worked hard for us and we loved her for it.

Sometimes I think we were cruel to her, but she suffered it all. She had a little brown, seventeen-year-old mongrel dog called Tess that slept most of the time on a little stool in the corner of the dining room. Tess was incontinent and often leaked onto the carpet. Particularly in winter, when all windows were kept tightly closed, the dining room would smell a bad doggy smell, especially noticeable when coming in from the fresh air. I will admit that we tormented that little dog that Mrs. Reeve loved so much. The dog was still alive when I left the house in 1963.

Mrs. Reeve was an avid fan of wrestling and would never miss her Saturday afternoon's entertainment in front of the television. She was a Catholic, but I don't remember her going to church on Sundays. Pope John XXIII died during my stay there. I remember clearly how much she thought of him, and how sad she was the day he died.

Mr. Reeve was a stocky, grey-haired Londoner of sixty years. He had been a builder before falling off a ladder some years before, severely damaging his back. He had a little van, which he parked in the front garden. He hobbled about, and was not able to do much physical work. He therefore spent much of the time at home. This must have been the reason why Mrs. Reeve decided to take in lodgers. In 1962, Mr. Reeve died in Lewisham Hospital of a heart-related illness at the age of sixty-two. I remember going to see him in the hospital shortly before he died. He lifted the bedclothes and showed me his private parts, which were swollen. He seemed to take his illness very lightly. It was the last time I saw him alive.

I will never forget the day they brought his body home. His coffin was placed in the front sitting room for about two days, for friends and relations to come to pay their last respects. That night, I went to the pub next door, the St. German's Hotel, with some of the boys. On returning to the house, having probably consumed at least two pints of beer, we decided to take a look at Mr Reeve in his coffin. Mrs. Reeve had gone to bed. We crept into the sitting room and drew back the lace cover. The smell of the preservative that is used to disguise the odour of decay is what I remember most about the escapade. Mr. Reeve was very pale and serene. I think it was the first dead body I had ever seen in my life.

We boys often went to the St. German's Hotel in the evening after dinner. We hardly ever reached the stage of being drunk, but I do recall one night, when I had to be helped home, having been very sick. On that evening, we had gone to other pubs in the area. I must have spent more money than I should have done on beer and cigarettes, for I had also picked up the smoking habit. Many times, I tried to kick the addiction, without success, until I got married, when I finally gave it up, never to smoke regularly again.

Mrs. Reeve was mildly disapproving of our drinking escapades, but never became angry, when we trooped in from the pub after closing time. If she had not retired to bed, she would pretend to be cross. 'You dirty old stop-outs!' she would normally say, but you could always detect a smile behind the frown.

Mrs. Reeve appeared to recover from her husband's death very quickly. She went on with her hard work, for her four guineas a week per boy. There were four at any one time. She cannot have made much money, judging by the amount of food we consumed, but I believe she did what she did for the love of it as much as for the financial reward, and they owned the house. The top floor was rented separately, but I never went up there. Two boys shared the first-floor front room; the best room in the house, and there were two single rooms, one on the ground floor next to the sitting room with a window overlooking the back garden and one on the first floor immediately overhead. The Reeves slept in the back bedroom. Curiously, the only bathroom in the house led off their bedroom, so that we boys had to pass through their room to reach it. Very often, we had to tiptoe past their sleeping forms if we were late coming home; a strange arrangement, to be sure!

At first, I shared the front bedroom with a medical student called John. He was a shy, tall and lanky boy with straw coloured hair. He told me that each medical student was allocated a body by the hospital at the start of the training course, and this body was kept in formaldehyde, to be removed for dissection when needed. I was rather happy to be studying accountancy and not medicine!

Of the other young men who shared those dinners and pub evenings, there was a South African dental student by the name Tony Skinner, who stayed a short time. There was Brian Fletcher, a Manxman, who worked in insurance. He was one of Mrs. Reeve's most persistent teasers, and the dog's too! John Dangerfield considered himself a cut above the rest of us. He didn't mix much, and scorned our trips to the pub. Bill Davidson was the best friend I had there. He was a Glaswegian, training to be a draughtsman. He was going out with a Jewish girl from Hornsey in North London. Linda had a friend, also a Jewess, called Miriam, and the four of us went out together a few times. Miriam was a thin, sweet girl. Our most memorable date was the evening I took her out to the Odeon, Marble Arch, to see *Lawrence of Arabia*. The film had just been released. It must have been 1962. After the film, she took me to her parents' home in Leytonstone in East London, where I had a bed for the night. After leaving Forest Hill in 1963, I never saw her again. She was the first girl I went out with. I had had one other experience before this. I forget how I met the girl and also her name. She invited me to her house for the evening. Her parents had gone out, and we spent the evening sitting on the settee, cuddling and kissing. I was a novice with the opposite sex at that time. I must have disappointed her. I never saw her again.

Brian Instance had a room in Mrs. Reeve's house for a while. He was an accounts clerk earning a decent salary, with a Mini and coins in his pocket for a pint and a fag. Our excursions were invariably restricted to the pubs of South London, and I eventually got bored with his company. The two of us splashed out one Easter, motoring over to Paris in his car for a long weekend. It was before I learnt how to drive. He thought he had some of Stirling Moss's blood in his veins! I cannot forget the experience of careering round the *Arc de Triomphe* in Brian's Mini, along with a few hundred crazy French drivers, fortunately in the same direction as they! We stayed in a cheap but clean *pension* and drank cheap but palatable wine in pavement cafes, and Brian smoked too many cigarettes for his own good, as he always did. When I knew him as a young man, he already suffered from a bad smoker's cough.

I only remember one party during those Forest Hill days. It was held in a neighbour's house. Aretha Franklyn's song, 'Killing me softly' was very popular just then. Bill took Linda and her fat cousin called Judy. It was intensely boring. I got paired off with the cousin. She got herself worked up, but I was not able to raise any enthusiasm at all. She was not my type. What *was* my type? There was a girl who lived not far away who had the most beautiful eyes; in fact, everything about her was beautiful. I think her name was Hazel…or was that the colour of her eyes? I believe it was both. She was definitely my type. But I was an immature boy, and I would have had to summon up monumental courage to ask her out. Perhaps I would have benefited from attending a mixed school, rather than an all-boys boarding school, where there were few opportunities to learn how to relate to the opposite sex.

I made friends at TMcL. Occasionally, we would meet after work, spending the evening in the City or the West End. Money was tight for us, so we would look out for the cheaper eating places. One evening, we went to the East End, to a very famous Chinese restaurant, where the food was truly delicious, and you could still fill your stomach to the brim for less than a pound. On one of these evenings out, I missed the last train back to Forest Hill. Taxis were outside the range of my budget. My only alternative was to walk the seven or eight miles home in the middle of the night. In those days, we never gave a thought to personal security: the streets of London were still safe. But the distance on hard pavements was a daunting prospect. A taxi driver quoted me £6, (one-and-a-half week's full board)! I set out to walk. I must have reached halfway, when I weakened and decided to hail the black cab.

One year, Bill Davidson invited me to his parents' home in Glasgow for the Hogmanay celebrations; a serious business in Scotland. Before England made New Year's Day a holiday, Scotland had *two* days to celebrate, on the basis that you had to have another day to recover from the alcoholic binge that is more or less compulsory north of the border. Bill's parents' home was a cramped apartment in a drab tenement, in a dingy part of the City. In common with most other males on New Year's Eve, we made the rounds of the local bars; dimly lit, dirty, sawdust-strewn drinking dens. A glass of 'heavy' beer would accompany a tot of Scotch whisky, which is knocked back in one gulp. This is followed by another beer, and so on. Drunkenness was, and possibly still is, a common phenomenon in the largest City in Scotland. By midnight on New Year's Eve, most people are well oiled. The first visitor after midnight brings a gift of coal, to bring good luck to the house. It is called 'First-footing'. Auld Lang Syne, with words by Scotland's revered poet, Robbie Burns, is sung in a circle by the members of the household, to welcome in the New Year. Needless to say, no one, apart from those providing essential services, rises early on the first day of January!

Bill was a fervent fan of Glasgow Rangers, the top team in Scottish League football at that time. Every New Year's Day, Rangers met their bitter rivals, Glasgow Celtic, on the football field at Ibrox Park, and perhaps this tradition still survives. But this was more than friendly football rivalry. The Presbyterian Scots supported Rangers, while the Catholic immigrants from Ireland supported Celtic, the team that played in Irish green. This was religious fanaticism, mirroring in microcosm the sectarian animosity that had plagued the Emerald Isle for decades, and which was to erupt into a war of terror in the late 1970's. The football match was well policed, and glass bottles and alcohol strictly prohibited inside the ground. Rangers' supporters cheered, or jeered, depending on the way the game was going, from one side of the pitch, while the rival fans did the same from the other end. The supporters entered and exited from different gates, but in spite of this segregation, there was often violence outside the ground. I forget which team won on the day I was there.

In the evenings, I used to study at a big table in the spacious front bedroom at St. German's Road. I was taking a correspondence course with the School of Accountancy. It was hard to drag myself to that table on dark winter evenings. The house had no central heating, which meant thick sweaters and socks to avoid frostbite! It also took me some time to get to grips with the principles of double-entry bookkeeping. How is it possible that an asset can be on the same side as a loss, and a liability on the same side as a profit? One of our firm's partners made it very clear to me early on in my training, by telling me that the debit side was always on the side nearest the window! I suspect the partner enjoyed the same joke with each articled clerk who came along! But seriously, we have to thank Napoleon Bonaparte for the double-entry system that is used worldwide, and almost exclusively in bookkeeping. And what an ingenious system it is too! Its perfection has always amazed me. And difficult as it appeared at first, it turned out to be simple to understand.

The founder of the firm, Thomson McLintock, was killed in a road accident in East Africa, but I have no idea what he was doing there. A junior relation had his name on the notepaper, but I never met him. The senior partner at the time that I joined the firm was a dour, ancient Scotsman called Robert Lister. He had an equally ancient secretary, who was a fanatical

Jehovah's Witness. William Slimmings was at that time well down the list, but he later became the senior partner, and was knighted for his services on some important Government body or other. Thomson McLintock & Co no longer exists. Mergers and takeovers have all but wiped out the smaller audit firms, creating colossal multinational firms, with offices around the globe.

I commuted to the City by train from Honour Oak, the station next up the line from Forest Hill. From London Bridge Station, I joined the human river flowing over London Bridge, while the Thames flowed underneath. Everyone would be heading for a day's work in one of the thousands of offices centred in that hub of financial activity. The City was, and still is, an important international centre for banking services, insurance, stockbroking and shipping, among others. At the end of the day, the human river flows the other way, and silence reigns until the next morning. Incredibly, the resident population of The City was barely six thousand. With the new Dockland developments, thousands more have joined.

The office of Thomson McLintock occupied the first building in King William Street, on the left and just across the bridge. It was a mere five minutes' walk to the building in Leadenhall Street, where my grandfather had spent the whole of his working life. Incidentally, after I ceased to work in Thomson McLintock's London office, the old London Bridge was dismantled, stone by stone, sold to an American billionaire and shipped across the Atlantic, to be re-erected somewhere in the USA. A new bridge now stands in its place.

How many different bridges have linked the City with the South Bank of the River Thames since that spot was first settled? When the Romans first founded the walled city of Londinium in the First Century BC, a stone bridge was constructed over the river, to link the south coast ports, from which Roman galleys crossed the narrow strait to Gaul, and finally to Rome. Roman structures were made to last, so it is likely that their bridge stood as a monument long after the fall of the Roman Empire. But in 1209, a new, single-span bridge was constructed a little downstream from the current bridge, at a narrow point in the river. At that time, the river was not bounded by artificial embankments, and in places spread itself more than a thousand feet wide. Because of the narrowness at that particular point, 'shooting the bridge' was a risky business. Eventually, out of this grew the saying that London Bridge was built 'for wise men to cross over and for fools to pass under.' In time, the bridge became a veritable city in itself, and what a sight it must have presented! In Shakespeare's time, over a hundred wooden shops and other businesses were crowded on top, some as much as six stories high, leaning precariously over the water and shored up by rickety struts. At the southern end, one would witness the heads of traitors and other criminals stuck on top of poles, as a warning to others who might be tempted to play games with the authorities of the day.

In Elizabethan times, the entire City of London was situated on the north bank of the river, surrounding the 11th Century Tower of London, where many opponents of the Crown languished for years, or awaited execution. Entirely walled, occupying the incredibly small area of 448 acres and boasting over a hundred parishes, each with its parish church, the City was crowded, rat-infested and totally lacking in sanitation. It consisted almost entirely of wooden buildings. The common practice of hanging upper floors over the street meant that one could almost touch one's neighbour. It also made streets dark and airless, and hotbeds of squalor and disease. All known diseases made life there a nightmare, and life expectancy did not exceed thirty-five years. The Plague was the deadliest disease of all, carrying off tens of thousands of souls during an outbreak. An epidemic was certain to rear its feared head at least once every ten years. All theatres and other public gatherings, with the notable exception of church services, were forbidden within seven miles of the City during these times. Drunkenness in those days was rife and brawls were common. The authorities attempted to contain the situation by imposing a dusk-to-dawn curfew, and by closing the various gates into the City at night. All in all, London was not the relatively safe environment I experienced during my young working life!

Great strides have been made in recent years in reducing environmental pollution in London. Fish swim once more under London Bridge, as they did in Shakespeare's time, when dace, barbell and an assortment of shellfish were plentiful. On my way to the office in the 1960's, I crossed a river in which no fish could survive. Another interesting point about the Thames was the regular winter fairs that took place upon the frozen river during both Elizabethan and Victorian times, testifying to the severity of English winters. I remember only one year in which the Thames froze over completely: that was in the winter of 1962/63. Even then, I believe it was not cold enough for the river as far downstream as the City of London to freeze over, let alone producing ice thick enough to support a fair, and the multitudes that must have thronged the event.

In the 16th Century, the City, taken together with neighbouring Westminster, and Southwark on the south bank of the river, was the third greatest city in Europe, after Paris and Naples, with a population exceeding two-hundred-thousand. The reason for this was the steady influx of fortune seekers from the Provinces and Protestant refugees from Catholic Europe. However, much of the City and its environs consisted of squalid slums.

Close to the southern bank of the Thames, the famous Tabard Inn still stands. The Inn was featured in Geoffrey Chaucer's late 14th Century epic poem, 'The Canterbury Tales', from where a band *'wel nine and twenty'* pilgrims began their long journey to Canterbury,

'the hooly blisful martyr for to seke,
That hem hath holpen whan that they were seeke.'

It was also in Southwark, only a hundred feet from the river, where the famous Globe Theatre was built in 1598 by a theatre company partly owned by Shakespeare.

The City of London was almost entirely made of wooden buildings until 1666, when a raging fire destroyed it entirely. It was a blessing in disguise. The City had been hit by an outbreak of the deadly Plague the year before, during which, people died like flies. The Great Fire of London dealt the Plague a fatal blow, with almost no loss of life, and allowed a more modern and healthier city to spring up from the ashes. Just opposite our office stands The Monument, a column marking the spot where the fire started in a small bakery in Pudding Lane. During one lunch hour, I climbed the steep spiral stone steps to the caged platform for a view out over the City. I inherited my father's fear of heights, and was glad to return to ground level. The cage must have been added after one or more stressed city workers preferred the short cut from the top to the street below!

My first few weeks in the office were spent in the checking department, which occupied a small room off the audit department. There I worked with a retired horseracing correspondent, Mr. Dickinson, who had worked for a The London Evening News. Our job was to read over sets of accounts. He would read from the hand-written proof, and I would check the typed version. Mistakes were referred back to the typing department for correction. There were no desktop computers then: simple no-memory electric typewriters were used, and corrections were made with a rubber or with Typex. Checking accounts was tedious work. I almost nodded off several times, especially after lunch. But the old man was patient, and we chatted to relieve the boredom. I got to know the typists. I and other clerks would occasionally take them out for drinks after work. Their choice of drinks was usually spirits, vodka and lime being the favourite, which meant I couldn't afford to do it too often! Finally, my stint in the checking department came to an end, and another articled clerk was hauled in to take my place. It was then that I started working in the audit department.

As I have written in Part I, Grandad Walker lost his younger brother to cancer one Christmas. Josie, the daughter of that brother, worked in the duplicating department of the firm and we got quite friendly. She was sixteen years old and lived in the Dockland area of London. Her father had worked there as a docker, an indicator to me of the level of society my grandfather had come from; not that it mattered to me that Josie was from a working-class family, as we used to say. I lost contact with her when I went off to Edinburgh, and she must have left the job before my return a year later. I sometimes wonder what my cousin is doing now; probably a grandmother. With my grandparents long gone, it would be hard to know how to contact her.

After reporting to work on Monday mornings, I would be told which audit team I would join that week. The firm had many large clients, which meant I could be several weeks working in one place. After the first day, it was normal to travel directly to the client's office from home. One of my first jobs was the head office of Imperial Chemical Industries Limited on Milbank. ICI was one of the largest UK companies. They had a punched-card computer system, and dozens of girls did nothing else but punch holes in cards, which were then fed into a reader and printed out. Used punched-cards occupied large storerooms, while the mainframe computer was housed in an enormous air-conditioned room. Checking reams of printed information was exceptionally monotonous. Just verifying a bank reconciliation could take a week! Finding a difference could take a very long time. The job required accuracy and concentration.

An audit team would mostly include a comptometer operator; without exception a woman. Like the job of a typist, it was considered work for a female. The comptometer was the equivalent of today's calculator; a huge metal box, the metal keys of which stood out like the keys of the old typewriters. The woman would expect the machine to be carried to her desk by a male junior clerk, because the comptometer was a very heavy thing for a woman to hump around. Columns of figures were added up by the comp. operator for days on end; a dreary job, for sure! At that time, account books were hand written, and mistakes and deliberate falsification of totals was a real danger. Now that financial records are computerised, the comptometer operator has probably become extinct like the dinosaurs. However, having a young girl on the audit team livened up the atmosphere. Articled clerks at that time; strangely perhaps, were almost all men. On small audits, the junior clerk would usually check the castings. I remember one audit senior castigating me early in my career, for saying I could not add a long column of figures. But I mastered the art and I am grateful for the training. It amuses me now to see people having to use the calculator on their mobile phone to add two figures together!

There were other more interesting audits. In the severe winter of 1962/63, I was part of a small team auditing a company near Tonbridge in Kent. I had two wheels by then in the form of a Lambretta scooter, but with icy roads, it was a daunting journey early on the Monday morning. During our lunch hour, we would skate on a nearby frozen river. Another time, during a particularly hot summer spell, I had to attend a stock-take in the West End. The job required long hours, and I stayed in a very smart hotel in Russell Square. It was so hot at night it was almost impossible to sleep. The temperature shot up to 94 degrees Fahrenheit, (32 degrees Celsius) during the day. Another time, I commuted to Croydon. The audit was incredibly boring. In a few days I was due to start my Kuwait holiday. I counted the minutes to coffee break, and then to lunchtime, after which I allowed myself a cigarette. I was trying desperately to cut down at that time; a futile exercise!

Away from the office on audit, I would normally eat lunch alone. It was almost always half a pint of bitter and a porkpie. Apart from smoking, I was addicted to Mars bars, and I would sometimes enjoy both addictions after lunch. If I were flush, I would often buy an apple, to scrape away the sugar from my teeth. Companies with free canteens would always be welcome, since we were treated like employees. But the top honour was to be invited to join the top management in the executive dining room, where the food was usually good, and plentiful enough to send us into a doze in the afternoon!

During those first three years, the work was routine, and I was given little responsibility. It was a life of 'ticking'. We used to say, 'ours is not to reason why: ours is just to tick and die!' In 1961, I took the first of the five examinations and passed. In 1962, I failed in one subject of Part II and had to repeat the exam in 1963.

It must have been in 1961 that I bought that new Lambretta motor scooter for about £150. I must have taken it on hire purchase, because with my salary of not much more than £250 per year and £15 a month from my father, I could not have afforded to buy it with cash. It was my first taste of mobility and I made the most of it. At that time, Nanna and Grandad Hawley were still living in Green Harbour, and often at weekends I would wrap myself up in waterproof jacket, gloves, crash helmet and goggles, and in winter an extra sweater, waterproof trousers and gumboots as well, and set off early on

Saturday morning for the Berkshire countryside. Mum had bred in me the delights of early rising. The English have a wise saying. 'Early to bed, early to rise, makes a man healthy, wealthy and wise.'

Apart from the five-mile Preston By-pass, which had opened in 1958, Britain had no motorways until the M1 from London to Birmingham opened in 1961. It was some years before the M4 motorway from London to Bath and South Wales was built, so my scooter ride took me along the South Circular Road to Hammersmith, along the busy A4 to Reading, and then by the A439 to Pangbourne. A final three-mile ride up the hill brought me to Upper Basildon. Nanna always gave me a welcome, as well as a strong cup of tea. Nanna's tea was always so strong you could almost stand a spoon in it! I was not fond of stewed tea.

Dennis and Midge, (Dad's younger and only sister), were frequent visitors to Green Harbour while her parents lived there, and they often stayed for the weekend. Dennis was still a Betterware salesman and worked hard during the week. Television was a regular Saturday night entertainment at Green Harbour. Variety shows, quizzes and contests were popular programmes. I was not keen on that type of show, but I would sit with them for company. Dennis was always voluble in front of the TV set, forever commenting and joking about the antics going on upon the screen.

I am hazy about daytime activities, but there would usually be jobs to be done in the garden. By that time, Grandad had not the health to do much heavy work. But walking around the area was my favourite pastime. I had become interested in birds, (the feathered kind!), and would enjoy sitting in a wood, listening to their sounds, and the sudden flitting of wings, flapping in the case of the pigeons and doves. The sight of the red head of a woodpecker, or the related tree creeper, hopping around a tree trunk looking for insects, would be a bonus, as would be the moving song of the illusive nightingale.

It must have been in 1961 or 1962 that Nanna and Grandad moved from Green Harbour, due to his failing health. His daughter, Midget and husband, Dennis were living in Harwell, and it was there that Nanna and Grandad moved.

The Lambretta took me to many places. I went visiting my maternal aunts and uncles and cousins; Eileen in Petts Wood, Doreen in Beckenham, Dorothy in Rickmansworth and Michael in Blackheath. Eileen and Doug had lived in 9, St. Francis Close for many years. Later, they moved to Faversham in Kent. Eileen must have become a magnet, because Michael also went to live in that town. Later, Doreen and Geoffrey, after a stint in Oman, moved to the little village of Bourton under Blean, not far away.

During my parents' 1962 leave, I took a few days off work, and rode the scooter to Devon, where they had hired and parked a caravan on the land that Dad had bought two years before. The clearest memory of that holiday is the severe sinusitis I suffered. I sat in the caravan with my sinuses swollen so badly I could hardly see from my left eye. Memories of Dad's leave are few. But cine films remind me that a week was spent sailing on the Norfolk Broads in 'Brigand.' Of this holiday I recall little.

Auntie Dorothy and Uncle John moved to Rickmansworth in Hertfordshire from Mottingham just before I started working in the City. I clearly remember my first visit to the new house, a short time after commencing work, standing on the doorstep in my smart City regalia. I enjoyed going there. Dorothy was one of my favourite aunts. My brother John and I had stayed with her in Mottingham, after our parents went out to Kuwait to live in 1955. Uncle John was a good man, but as I have said before, he was someone who found it difficult to get on with something, and this drove his wife crazy. Soon after moving to the new detached house in a quiet neighbourhood, from where Uncle John commuted by train to his office, he started to make some alterations to the kitchen. For years after, whenever I went there, the work on the kitchen would not have been completed. Dorothy lived in that house as a widow, until she passed away in her mid-eighties. John had passed on some years before. Her two children were married and lived far away; Colin in Scotland and Janet in Cornwall, but they had always been a close family, and they kept faithfully in contact with their mother in her final years.

I have a vivid memory of one very foggy day in early 1963, when I scooted over to Blackheath, not more than five miles from Forest Hill.

Michael had recently married, and was living in a flat with his wife, Ann and baby daughter. I had been his best man at their wedding in Cheshire in 1962. It was the journey home from Blackheath that has stuck in my memory. As it got dark, the fog thickened to the consistency of soup, making it almost impossible to see the way forward. Fortunately, I made it home to Forest Hill without mishap. Even more than eight years after the passing of the Clean Air Act, London could still produce a pea-souper. Michael and Ann split up soon after that. Michael had another three marriages, mainly stormy ones, and a life on and off the bottle. I only saw him once or twice after that visit in 1963, but news of him came via Auntie Eileen. I was told that he rode around Faversham on a bicycle with a motor. For some reason he missed family reunions that were attended by his sisters and elder brother. He died in 2011 at the age of seventy-two from emphysema, after a lifetime of heavy smoking.

During that exceptionally cold winter of 1962/63, I was occupying the single room on the first floor of the Reeve's House. The house had no heating, and the waste pipe of the wash basin in my room was frozen solid for about six weeks, together with a few inches of water in the basin. That winter, I contracted pleurisy and spent at least a week in bed. It was the winter that claimed the life of my Dad's father. It was also the winter that the River Thames at Lower Basildon froze over, something I had never seen, and have not seen since.

The cold weather arrived suddenly on Boxing Day 1962. Mum was in England that Christmas, and Bill Davidson was spending a few days with us at Green Harbour. We were out walking in the lanes towards Yattendon, when the snow began to fall. It was a gift to us, but then it was to snow for the next few days. Mum records in her diary that it snowed heavily on New Year's Day. On the 3rd January she wrote, 'Ice everywhere. Rain has fallen and frozen on every twig and blade of grass, lovely sight, never seen anything like it before.' A foot of snow lay in our front garden, and it was sealed in by a thick layer of ice that remained for weeks. Mum left for Kuwait on the 19th January 1963. For the first two weekends in January, I had taken the train to Pangbourne on Friday evenings and back to London on Monday mornings, going straight to the office from Paddington. It was on Saturday the 12th January that we received the news of Grandad's death. Mum records that she wired Dad in Kuwait. Nowadays, a simple and costless WhatsApp call would be made. In 1963, a visit to the Post Office to send a telegram was the mode of communicating news. Mum represented him at the funeral.

Dad's home leave had been taken in even years up to 1962, and so it was a surprise to read in Mum's diary that he was in England on leave in 1963, from the 4th April to the 12th May. I was saving my leave for a holiday in Kuwait in the summer, but I travelled to Upper Basildon for weekends, either by train or on the Lambretta. That Easter, we drove to Devon in a hired car and visited our old haunts, including the land that Dad had bought, and on which he dreamt he would one day build a house. It was that weekend, the diary tells me, that we learnt that planning permission had been refused by the local authority, since it was agricultural land. The agent, who should have known that permission would be declined, was instructed to put the property on the market. We were disappointed, but when I look back at later events, principally the purchase of Yew Cottage, in which Mum and Dad spent many happy years, I know it was for the best. Devon was where we spent some wonderful holidays, but it was far from home territory.

Our trips to Devon, or any holiday destinations, were always exciting. Determined to beat the traffic, we would get up at the crack of dawn, pack up the car and set off before 5 am. We would be half way there by breakfast time, when we would enjoy sandwiches and a flask of tea, or we would stop at a roadside café, and tuck into a cooked breakfast. You can tell the best transport cafes by the number of lorries parked outside! After leaving school in 1961, my brother, John enrolled in the Oxford College of Architecture. One holiday, he had been given a project to complete by a fixed deadline, and on the night before we were due to start the holiday, John was frantically working to finish his drawing. The rest of the family retired to bed, but John worked throughout the night. We drove off early in the morning, John without a wink of sleep. At that time, The Beatles LP called 'A Hard Day's Night' was in the charts, and it became our signature tune for that trip.

> *It's been a hard day's night: I've been workin' like a dog;*
> *It's been a hard day's night: I should be sleepin' like a log.*

I only had one scrape with the Law in those scooter riding days. It was before I took my riding test. It was a requirement to display 'L' plates on the back and front of the scooter. I must have lost the back plate, because a policeman stopped me to ask for my licence. I had to attend Woolwich Magistrates Court and pay a fine.

As part of my apprenticeship, I had to spend one year at a Scottish university, after passing Part II of the Institute's examinations. This I did on the second attempt in June 1963. After enjoying my last holiday in Kuwait in the summer of 1963, I said goodbye to Mrs. Reeve and my fellow boarders, and prepared to start my year at Edinburgh University. It was to be an interesting and exciting year, and it started in an utterly unexpected manner, as I am about to relate.

What a good idea it would be to have my scooter in Edinburgh! And what fun it would be to ride it the four-hundred miles from London to the Scottish capital! Those were the exciting ideas that filled my mind in early October 1963. I was full of confidence as I set off on my journey, the minimum of luggage strapped to the back of the Lambretta. I had no fixed plan, preferring to stop when I became tired, and arrive when I arrived. Having started early, and stopping frequently to ease the discomfort in my back, I reached Catterick, a neat little town in Yorkshire, noted for its Army camp. There I slept the night in a small hotel.

Suitably refreshed and with renewed confidence, I began the second day of riding. The weather was cool but dry, and I was well wrapped up. I reached the border with Scotland at Berwick-on-Tweed; a small, grey stone town, stopping at a pub for a snack and a small beer. I did not know at that time that Berwick was going to be the end of the ride for me. I left the pub, knowing that only sixty miles lay between me and my destination. It was drizzling as I rode slowly through the town. Suddenly, a van pulled out from a side turning and came towards me. The driver cannot have been looking where he was going. I applied the brake and the wheels skidded on the wet road. The next few minutes were a confused jumble of sensations. I hit the front of the van and landed on my knees on the road. It was fortunate that I was wearing jeans, a pair of thick waterproof trousers and wellington boots, otherwise the damage might have been greater. I was taken by ambulance to the local hospital, where they decided I would need an operation, and Edinburgh Royal Infirmary was the place for that. The Lambretta was taken away by the police. It was a write-off and I never saw it again.

In later years, my father considered suing the driver of that van; a Mr. Washington. In the end, we decided to drop it and forget about it. I have no doubt we could have got damages for a lifetime of living without a kneecap, but I am glad we did not pursue the matter. It was the driver's fault, but was there a remote possibility that, had I not had that accident, I would have had a more serious accident later on, leading to death instead of injury?

So, I entered Scotland in an ambulance, rather than on a scooter as I had intended. I had shattered my left kneecap and severely bruised the other one. I didn't know then that months were to go by before I would be able to walk properly.

EDINBURGH UNIVERSITY

MY FIRST TWO DAYS IN Scotland were spent in that famous hospital; Edinburgh Royal Infirmary, where I underwent an operation to remove the pieces of bone from my left knee, and had my whole leg encased in plaster. After that, I was transferred to the Astley Ainslie Hospital, a very pleasant nursing home on the very edge of Edinburgh, south of Morningside, with a view of the Pentland Hills. It was another two weeks before I was discharged. During that time, I celebrated my 22nd birthday. I must have written to Kuwait to break the news of my accident, and perhaps I received a card from my parents. Nowadays, a mobile phone call would have been the simple solution.

It was by no means a disagreeable fortnight. The nursing staff was wonderful, the ward was bright, and the view of gardens and hills was delightful. I made friends with a nurse and we met a few times later. She was an orphan, having lost both her parents in a car accident. She had been thrown out of the car into a field and had been unharmed. She was a very sweet Scottish girl, little and plump. I must have had visitors; perhaps the boys from the London office, who were starting University at the same time. I remember the man in the bed opposite. His leg had been amputated, but he could still feel it. He had to remember, when getting out of bed, that he could not put the leg he thought he had, but he didn't have, on the floor.

Edinburgh is a beautiful and ancient city, built of stone. Its famous castle, built in the 11th Century by King Malcolm III, occupies pride of place on a rocky, volcanic peak in the centre, overlooking Princes Street to the north, where the fashionable shops are located. Just south of the castle lay one of the oldest parts of the City, composed of sombre stone tenement buildings and cobbled streets. Beyond those were the Universities of Edinburgh and Herriot Watt, and the teaching hospital. To the east, the Royal Mile leads to the Palace of Holyrood, the official residence of the Royal Family. It is along, or near the Royal Mile, that the majority of the population lived in the tall stone tenement buildings, up to fourteen stories high, dating from around, or after the 15th Century. It was here that the mainly Irish immigrant workers were housed during the Industrial Revolution. To the north of Princes Street lie two more, narrower parallel streets, before the land drops sharply down to less salubrious neighbourhoods. It is there, in Henderson Row, that I was to live until the University year ended in June 1964. Beyond the northern reaches of the City lay the Firth of Forth and the port of Leith.

Edinburgh is the capital of Scotland, with a population of about 550,000, the second largest city in Scotland. Glasgow, on the other hand, is the industrial and commercial centre of the Country, with a major shipbuilding industry, and a population of one-point-seven million. But my Glaswegian friend, Bill was fond of pointing out that the only good thing to come out of Edinburgh is the train for Glasgow! To them, Edinburgh folk are stuck up. The dislike is mutual however. Edinburgh people consider Glaswegians to be an inferior class.

By the time I was discharged from the hospital, my future flat-mates had found accommodation, and were well established on the ground floor of the drab stone block in an equally drab street. There were seven of us from TMcL London office who had enrolled for the course. I shared with three others; Michael Crabtree, Chris Pettman and Michael Denison, while Bill Lawes and Hugh Stewart shared a flat in Morningside, an up-market neighbourhood on the other side of the University. Another young man, Peter Morris, lived in digs alone.

Mike Crabtree was by far the most brilliant of the bunch, which was not saying much, because I think we were not the brightest stars of the office! He was a Mathematics graduate from Cambridge University. He hardly found the need to study, due to his photographic memory. He could read a page from the book and would not forget it. It was jealousy that made him the brunt of many taunts from Mick Denison and Chris Pettman. He had a reputation for not being able to hold his beer, an unfortunate disability in student-company. He qualified a couple of years before I did. Having a degree, he completed his exams in three years, as opposed to those of us who entered the profession straight from school. He went on to become a partner in Thompson McLintock & Co. We remained friends, and once back in London we saw each other frequently.

Chris Pettman, an ex-public-school boy, was the son of a stockbroker in the City of London. The family was well off and lived in the Stockbroker Belt in Surrey, together with hundreds of other stockbroker families. I shared a bedroom with him. He had a habit of sniffing, and we reminded him of it many times. After leaving the firm in 1967, I was not to see Chris again.

Michael Denison was also from a wealthy family, and spoilt too. He ran a new, yellow, open-top Triumph TR4, complete with overdrive; a popular sports car of the 1960's. On the meagre salary of an articled clerk, he could not possibly have been able to afford to run a car at all, but Mick obviously had other income. He shared with Chris the public-school accent. We used to hare around the countryside in his car at the weekends. He became friends with a young publican, who ran a pub we used to frequent, some miles from the City. He owned an E-Type Jaguar coupe, the last word in sports cars for the lovers of speed at that time. It was capable of 140 mph. We admired that car. I never knew what happened to Mick after University. I imagine he was destined for the City. The 'old school tie' was a powerful introduction.

Bill Lawes and Hugh Stewart were good friends. I didn't know Bill well, but Hugh was a good friend of mine. He was the only son of older parents, and had the biggest inferiority complex I have ever known. He was short and dressed poorly. He considered himself ugly and incompetent. He had a sense of humour, but behind that lay a very unhappy soul. His father had been the Financial Director of a major UK company, but had already retired. He expected great things from his son, but the son thought he had no hope of living up to his father's expectations. On a lighter note, and one that demonstrates Hugh's sense of humour, I will never forget the small incident that took place in the lift in the London office. The office lift was a cage that grated and groaned its way up the seven floors, jerking to a halt at each stop. Hugh and I were returning to the office after lunch, and we shared the lift with two typists, one of whom had bought a pear, which she clutched to her bosom. Hugh suddenly said, 'Oh! What a lovely pair (pear)'! We could hardly keep straight faces. I don't think the girls saw the joke. If they did see it, they did not let on!

Peter Morris was a devout Christian and a regular churchgoer. He did not join the rest of us on our rowdy outings that would normally involve drinking in the Edinburgh bars. He persuaded me to go along with him to church one Sunday. I may have gone two or three Sundays in a row. Why did I stop? One Sunday, returning to the flat with Peter, and seeing my others flat mates there, I was ashamed of my 'holier than thou' feeling. I questioned my motives for going to church, and decided it was out of a false sense of spiritual superiority. I never went again. Peter was not popular with the others, but he was a very disciplined and focused young man. He went on to become a partner in the firm.

We had few close friends outside our London group, but one young Scottish lady by the name Leslie, who lived in a flat just around the corner with some other girls, was a source of rivalry between several of us. Hugh Stewart was utterly smitten by her, but Hugh, low in self-esteem, never succeeded in becoming close to her. Although Leslie was short and not the sexiest of females, she was very pretty, and had a lovely soft and calm disposition. I remember meeting her for a walk in Hyde Park after our year in Edinburgh.

One unofficial challenge that all students of the University 'were expected' to take up was to complete 'The Rose Street Mile.' Rose Street is a long, narrow street running parallel to, and to the north of Princes Street. It is famous for its profusion of bars; around twenty, I think. The challenge is to start at one end, have a drink in each bar on one side, and return on the other side, visiting each bar in turn. If you were still able to walk at the end, you had done 'The Rose Street Mile.' We would often go there at lunchtime for a glass of 'heavy' and a chicken pie. I never took up the challenge of 'The Rose Street Mile' and I was glad I did not succumb to it. But I still remember, and can even taste the delicious chicken pies!

Edinburgh is a cold and windy city; even cool in the summer, but especially from November to April. In calm winter weather, the mist would roll in off the North Sea, and chill us to the bone, even with electric fires in the bedrooms and an open fire. A grey mist would often spread itself over the City, and on the ground floor of the tenement building, it would be dark and dismal from early afternoon until well into the next morning.

I missed three whole weeks of lectures due to my accident. It was fortunate that Mick was able to take his car to the campus, for with a leg in plaster and crutches, it was not easy for me to get around. Six weeks after the operation, I had the plaster removed, and the chilling realisation struck me that my leg was thin, the muscles wasted, and I was unable to bend the knee at all. For the next few weeks, it was regular physiotherapy at the hospital. Forced bending, with the help of a nurse, was torment! Between sessions, I wore a half plaster, which allowed me to hobble around with my leg straight. Weeks went by and progress was slow.

What was happening in the world at that time? Plenty of changes. The cultural revolution was in full swing. In America, Bob Dylan was exciting the youth with his protest songs, and Martin Luther King made his unforgettable speech in Washington, in which he said, 'I have a dream that the sons of former slaves and the sons of former slave owners would sit together at the table of brotherhood.' In the UK, the BBC lifted the ban on mentioning sex, religion, politics and royalty on comedy shows.

It was the year of the first woman in space; the Cosmonaut Valentina Tereshkova.

It was the year of the Great Train Robbery, in which a gang stole over two-and-a-half-million pounds from a mail train. Some of the members of the gang, like Ronnie Biggs, were later to become celebrities.

The Beatles dominated the music scene with their hits, including 'She loves You,' and 'I want to hold your hand.' They had also issued two LP's, one of which, 'The Beatles,' was on everyone's Christmas shopping list that year. During that Christmas holiday, Chris Pettman gave a lavish party at his parents' Surrey home, and that Beatles record was worn out during the evening. I still wore the half-plaster, and had to sit out the dancing, however much I would have liked to have rocked to 'Roll over Beethoven!'

By far the most earth-shattering event of the year was the assassination of President John F. Kennedy on the 22nd November 1963. We were sitting before the fire in the flat that evening, when the news came over the radio. I remember well the headline in The Scotsman the next day.

They say that a dog is a man's best friend. This saying is supported by a true story from the 19th Century, about a dog's faithfulness that is truly Edinburgh's own. In the old part of the City, you will find a statue of a dog; Greyfriars' Bobby. The dog, a Skye terrier, belonged to John Gray, who worked for the police force as a watchman. In 1858, Gray died of tuberculosis, leaving his beloved dog behind. One version of the story goes that the creature never left his departed master's grave in Greyfriars Kirkyard, until the day he himself died fourteen years later. Another version claims that Bobby was fed daily by a sympathetic restaurateur. In 1867, it was decided that the dog should be put down, but the Lord Provost of Edinburgh paid the licence fee, and Bobby became the responsibility of the Edinburgh City Council. When Bobby died in 1872, he could not be buried in consecrated ground, but was interred just inside the gate of the Kirkyard, close to his former Master's grave. The stone monument stands testimony to that love and devotion. A wonderful and heartbreaking story!

Spring comes to Eastern Scotland late, but finally the weather improves sufficiently to allow a walk in the hills. On one such mild day in the spring of 1964, Mike Crabtree and I took a long walk in the Pentland Hills. I had finally discarded my half plaster, and walked with nothing but a bandage around my knee to give a little support. The physiotherapy had been of limited success. I was still unable to bend my knee very much. That walk in the hills was to change all that. We were descending a fairly steep slope through the heather, when my right leg slipped and I went down on my left leg, bending the knee forcibly. The pain was excruciating; far worse than the original accident. The knee swelled, and I had to be helped back to the car. For days, I could hardly move my leg at all, but slowly the swelling went, and I found to my amazement that I could bend my knee much more than before. That fall was a blessing in disguise. Today, I can run and perform most leg movements, but since the accident, I have never been able to put weight on the leg when bent: the muscles and tendons are weak. However, living without a kneecap has not been too difficult, except when a hard corner finds the fleshy part of the knee!

The summer term was the most enjoyable, because the better weather drew us into trips into the countryside. We joined many other residents on Arthur's Seat, a steep hill in the east, from which one sees the City spread out below. There was plenty of time for leisure activities, since the University course was hardly what one would call stressful. My flat-mates played golf, and I played once or twice.

The year came to an end with exams in Commercial Law, Economics and Accountancy, and certificates were presented to the successful candidates. We made our way back to London to complete our Articles in a very ordinary black, secondhand Hillman saloon car, which Chris Pettman had bought, and which we had serious doubts about its ability to make the distance. But it did, and we arrived in London safely. From then on it was four wheels for me, not two!

MUSWELL HILL

MUSWELL HILL IS A SUBURB of North London, to the east of Highgate, with Hendon close by on the other side. The nearest underground station is Highgate on the Northern Line, a fifteen-minute walk from Muswell Hill shops.

It was into a flat on the first floor of No. 2, Church Crescent that I moved on my return from Edinburgh in the summer of 1964. A young man from Hull, David Stead, was already ensconced in one single room when I moved in. I shared a room with another Yorkshireman. David Hurst was a big, bumbling rugby player. He loved his beer but not housework. He never lifted a finger to clean or tidy up after him. One day, we forced him to vacuum clean the flat, and he couldn't decide which way to hold the pipe, he was that hopeless! David Stead had a girlfriend called Yvonne, who lived a few doors away. She was older than he, and a more domineering woman I have never met. He was completely under her spell. I could never understand what he saw in her, but she had a power over him. The sitting room wallpaper was deeply scarred, and we came to know how it happened. One day, David had upset the girlfriend at breakfast time, and he had to take refuge behind the sitting room sofa, while she hurled dinner plate after dinner plate at the cowering boyfriend, splattering the wall with fried eggs, and leaving permanent indents in the wallpaper! He later moved in with her, and his place was taken by a fellow articled clerk in Thomson McLintock.

Ian van Rijn was Dutch. His parents lived in a house overlooking Lake

Geneva. Ian had been educated at Wellington College in Berkshire, and spoke English with a cultivated accent. We became very good friends. He had been born in what was at that time Dutch East Indies, until 1949, when it became Indonesia. When the Japanese overran the country during the Second World War, the family and baby Ian were put in a concentration camp, where they suffered deprivation and brutality. He was small as a result of malnutrition, and had a complex about it. He had a violent streak that was to manifest later. It was through him that I was to meet my wife of forty-six years.

I resumed work in King William Street, taking the tube from Highgate into the City. During fine weather, on the way to the station, I appreciated the walk through the peaceful park, where grey squirrels darted up and down and round and round the big plane trees lining the path, or scampered through the fallen leaves. If I happened to be working in the office, I would sometimes walk down Great Tower Street to the Tower of London. Nearby, there was an open area popular with speakers. One speaker who became famous was a Christian Minister, Trevor Huddleston, who worked to alleviate poverty. There were other speakers and showmen as well, who entertained the lunchtime crowds.

Normally, I would be working at the offices of the firm's clients. As more responsibility came my way, I was put in charge of small jobs, which meant supervising one or more junior clerks and the ubiquitous comptometer operator. Mostly, I worked under a qualified accountant as part of a team. Sometimes we worked out of town, which entailed staying in hotels during the week and travelling home on Friday afternoon. That was a new experience for me. It was also a time when I began to crawl out of my shell, plucking up the courage to chat up the girls in the clients' offices. I worked on an audit in Beaconsfield, which I remember for two reasons. I bought my first new car, a maroon Morris Mini Minor, HPP 923C, for £515 in the summer of 1965, and soon after that, I took out a very sweet waitress at the hotel. On the audit of Leicester Building Society, in the town of that name, I became friendly with a young typist called Jean Heal. She was pretty and sweet, and I took her address. But what was the point of keeping in touch with a girl in Leicester? On another audit in Wrexham in North Wales, I actually became brave enough to take out a girl with dazzling Welsh eyes. She was much older than I, and clearly more experienced. But I had my own car by then. We went out for a meal, and then kissed and cuddled in the car; very innocent stuff! Having your own car was a clear advantage, if you wanted to make it with the girls!

I made a big mistake with my first car, which I bought from a secondhand showroom just around the corner from the flat. I had taken a course of driving lessons, and had passed my test before leaving Edinburgh in June 1964. I was dying to become mobile. The salesman was a typical London secondhand car dealer; a smooth talker, and not above bending the truth if it suited him. I was not well off at that time, so I chose a second-hand Mini Minor, priced at £285. It was my first car and I was extremely excited, but it nearly killed me, and my uncle too! The car had obviously been in an accident. One day, on the motorway, a police car stopped me, and the officer told me the back wheels were not in line with the front wheels. I was committing no offence, but he said that I should know. I had not noticed! Shortly after this, I was proudly driving my Uncle Michael around the London streets. It was rare for us to be together. We came to a steep hill, at the bottom of which was a main road. I correctly applied the foot brake. The pedal sank softly to the floor, but the car continued to descend the hill. Before we knew it, we had crossed the main road, and mounted the opposite pavement. Fortunately, there had been no vehicle passing at the time. But I remember the white face of my uncle in the passenger seat. The lesson I learnt was not to trust London secondhand car dealers! I was told by someone that the brakes had been doctored with sawdust, to function for a short time, after which, failure was bound to occur. I traded that car in shortly after that for the new maroon Mini, which gave me wonderful service for four years.

The job I most enjoyed was the audit of a big factory in Dungannon, on the Northern Ireland side of the border with the Republic of Eire. This was in the days before sectarian violence erupted there, when Dungannon became the scene of fighting between the extremist terrorist group, The Irish Republican Army, fighting for an independent Ireland, (the Irish would call them freedom fighters), and the British Army. The town was a peaceful backwater in that autumn of 1965. I took my new car across the ferry from England or Wales, and drove to Dungannon. There are several ferries, and I forget which one it was. There were about six in the audit team, including one girl comptometer operator. Roger Brooks had his car, which meant we could all see Ireland during the weekends. We stayed in a very friendly hotel near the factory, right in the centre of Dungannon. Two female Irish receptionists joined us in off-duty hours, and we had fun gatherings. Weekday evenings would find us in the bar of the hotel, or partying in one of the bedrooms.

I was having such fun that my 24th birthday almost passed me by. I was busy working in the room set aside for the auditors. I remember that it was about 4pm, when I suddenly realised that it was the 20th October, my birthday. A most curious lapse! It had never happened before and it has never happened since.

Another incident sticks in my memory. I was down in the basement strong room, looking for certain documents, with the help of a young Irish girl. Alone in the cramped room, surrounded by shelves of files, I decided to make a pass at her. She was interested in my attentions but a little nervous. She wanted first to know if I were a Catholic. I think she was quite disappointed to hear that I was not. It was rather hot and stuffy down there, and the poor girl passed out in my arms. Was it because of the heat, or fear of my advances? Perhaps a little of each. However, she did forgive me for that, and for the fact that I wasn't a Catholic, and she did let me take her out one evening.

One weekend, the whole audit team drove to Dublin, the capital of Eire. I swear that I have never tasted draught Guinness like the one they serve there! They say it is due to the soft water from the River Liffey. I suppose they must purify the water first! As you can imagine, my drink during the seven weeks in Ireland was Guinness, and if it were not on tap, the bottled version. But nothing could compare with the Dublin draught brew; the original! It was so smooth, it slid down without seeming to touch the sides!

Another weekend was spent in County Down, where 'the mountains of Mourne sweep down to the sea,' to quote the song. On another occasion, we visited the North Coast of County Antrim, walking across the formation of hexagonal basalt columns of the Giant's Causeway. There is a similar formation on the West coast of Scotland, and a legend has it that they are the remains of a giant's bridge between Scotland and Ireland. In any case, the two sites have been geologically linked since pre-history. In the Antrim hotel, we played a record on the Juke box, until we practically wore it out. Minnie the Moocher was a song recorded by The Billy Cotton Band, and it became a signature tune for us, and we learnt it by heart. Some months later, I requested the record on Jimmy Young's BBC radio request programme, and dedicated it to the people I had shared a great time with in Ireland. My request was duly played, and I relived the weeks spent there. What memories!

Back in London, the routine of commuting to the City and life in Muswell Hill continued. At this time, Green Harbour was empty, and I would sometimes go down at the weekend for some fresh air. About this time, I had a surprise letter from a neighbour. The Sheldon family lived two doors away from Green Harbour. The husband had been killed in a train accident. It was his widow who wrote the letter, saying she was in love with my brother John and me, and would we meet her in a café in Reading for a cup of tea. We were curious, and took up the challenge. Mary must have been in her late thirties, while John and I were in our early twenties. Later, I met Mary without John. We kissed and petted in the front seats of my car. Fortunately, I stopped short of inviting her into the house. In later years, we would often see her walking in the village, and my parents thought she was very eccentric. I never told John or my parents about the brief encounter.

Two illnesses remain in my memory from this time. One day, the doctor was called to treat me for bronchitis. I thought his cough was a good deal worse than mine, and sure enough he passed away not long after! I sweated for what seemed like days in a camp bed in the sitting room of the flat. So severe was the fever that I hardly knew what was happening. I sweated buckets and the smell was overpowering. My sheets had to be changed every day, and I believe it was Yvonne, the dinner plate thrower, who changed them, and probably washed them too. She had positive attributes, to be sure! It must have been before I exchanged two legs for four wheels, because the weekend after my recovery, I invited a typist from the office to accompany me on a drive down to Green Harbour for the day in my parents' Wolseley, which they had decided to hang on to. Visits to England were becoming more frequent as the retirement date drew nearer. Mr. Fletcher of Theale Motor Works was put in charge of the car, and I was permitted to use it. I think the trip was a way of showing off! Mary Spooner lived in the East End of London, and her father was a dock worker. She was a fun girl, but she turned cool when I wanted a kiss in the sitting room of Green Harbour. Perhaps it was better that way!

I failed Part IV of the Accountancy examinations at the first attempt in June 1965. I had attended classes run by the Scottish Institute, but apart from that, I did little studying for the examination. My friends were mostly office colleagues, and we had some boozy outings in the West End. We made little use of the cultural treasure trove that London offered. A pity really! I came to appreciate this aspect of life later, when I was far from the centre of English culture. One night, I recall going out with the boys in Soho, the entertainment hub of the West End. Hugh Stewart and Bill Lawes were members of the drunken party. I will never forget how Charles Stewart disgraced himself, and us too. Sitting at the table in a restaurant, Charles was so sozzled that he vomited into his bowl of soup before he had started drinking it!

I kept up my friendship with Mike Crabtree, who lived with his parents in Pinner in Middlesex. One weekend, I stayed with him. His mother put us in one double bed. In the middle of the night, I felt someone touching me. It woke me up. When I moved, the hand was withdrawn immediately. I lay awake for some time, but he didn't touch me after that. I was relieved, because I was not sure how I would handle it. Later, he did get married, and when I was also married, he invited us to his house for dinner. He seemed to be a happy family man with children. It must be more than fifty years since I have seen him. I often wonder now if any of those comrades of the 1960's is still alive and kicking!

One winter evening, the Crabtree family had a party at home. Normally, I would stick to beer, but for some reason I decided to drink gin and dry

Martini; a fatal concoction. I drank six of these lethal mixtures that evening and had to drive home to Muswell Hill. Added to that, it was a bitterly cold winter night and the roads were icy. I can say that the tyres on that old Mini were not in the best condition. I am ashamed to say that I was not in a fit state to drive a car, but I arrived home safely. Breathalysers were later introduced, and automatic loss of a licence was imposed if one was caught driving with more than the set alcohol level in the blood. Britons took the change seriously and road accident deaths dropped markedly.

June Scott rented a room on the floor below our flat. I became friendly with her for a short time. Her parents lived in Cowley, a suburb of Oxford. She claimed to be a far-left-wing socialist and she was fond of discussing politics. Her favourite word was 'didactic'. I took her to the firm's dinner one year. Then she just left and I did not see her again.

I will never forget the state funeral of Sir Winston Churchill in 1965. No adult at that time was unaware of the tremendous debt the British people owed him for his leadership during those dark days of 1939 and 1940, when Britain had stood alone against the might of the German war machine. By 1940, practically the whole of Europe was under Nazi control. Now, the ninety-one-year-old Churchill was dead. I don't think any royalty has been given a more splendid sendoff in the whole history of England. The solemn and stately procession, attending the gun carriage, on which his flag-draped coffin sat, made its way from his home in Hyde Park Gate, through the West End, and through the City to the Tower of London, where it was loaded onto a barge for a ceremonious journey up the River Thames to Oxfordshire. Our office was just off Cheapside, and from the office we had a grandstand view of the whole procession. What was particularly incredible was that all the cranes that lined the river lowered their arms as the barge passed upriver. Churchill, descended from the Dukes of Marlborough, had refused a peerage, preferring to keep his seat in the House of Commons. He finally resigned as Prime Minister of Britain in 1955 at the age of eighty-one. His wish was to be buried in the churchyard of the village close to Blenheim Palace, the ancestral home of the Dukes of Marlborough. In later years, my wife, Margarita and I went to visit his grave. A simple stone marks the grave, bearing the words, 'Winston Spencer Churchill, 1874 – 1965.' Here was a man who, it could be said, saved Britain from defeat by Nazi Germany, had fought in the army in the Boer War, become an MP, and then First Lord of the Admiralty in 1911 at the age of thirty-seven. Suffering from Dyslexia as a child, he went on to become an accomplished writer of History, being awarded the Nobel Prize for Literature in 1953. He was also a gifted painter. Others would have accepted to be enshrined in Westminster Abbey with the famous and powerful. Churchill chose simplicity beyond imagination.

Ian van Rijn invited me to spend Christmas 1965 at his parents' home in Montreux, on the northern side of Lake Geneva. It was my first experience of Switzerland, and my debut on the ski slopes. In clear weather, the view from the house across the lake to the snow-covered mountains beyond was breathtaking. Ian's father had chains fitted to his car, to get a good grip on the icy roads. He drove us to the ski resort and collected us. Ian's parents were very hospitable, and I had a very pleasant time there. But despite our friendship, I never really got to know Ian in depth. There was always that hidden barrier between us. Perhaps that was as well, in view of what was to follow in 1966.

Ian van Rijn taught me how to enjoy 'real' coffee. Ian was a connoisseur, experimenting with the different blends, until he found one that suited his taste. He used paper filters. I must admit he made a 'mean' cup of coffee. It was a legacy he left with me, for we were soon to fall out! They say that 'all's fair in love and war!' Well, it was love and war that came to Muswell Hill early in June 1966. My life took an about-turn in that month. One of the most incredible moments of my life came out of the blue, utterly and completely unexpected. I will tell the story now.

MARGARITA GARCIA LOPEZ

IMAGINE THE SCENE. I AM alone in the flat one Saturday morning. Margarita arrives. She is Ian's girlfriend. While waiting for him, she sits at the table with an exercise book. She intended to do some English exercises. I look at it with her. Then, SNAP, the world is never the same again for me!!

I had met Margarita once before. It was on Saturday the 14th May 1966. I was spending the weekend at Green Harbour. Mum had already returned from Kuwait for good, and was living there. I arranged to meet Ian at a roadside pub, the Wagon & Horses, on the main A4 between Twyford and Maidenhead. It was roughly halfway between London and Upper Basildon. Ian wanted me to meet his Spanish girlfriend. Had he known the outcome, he would not have wanted us to meet. But he and I were friends, and it was natural for him to want to introduce us. John and I met them there and the four of us had a drink together.

Margarita was born in La Coruna, (now A Coruna), the regional capital of Galicia, in the far north-west of Spain. She was the only daughter of a highly respected dermatologist. Her mother had died in 1961, and her father had married again only two years later. Early in 1966, at the age of seventeen years, she went to stay with her father's cousin, Maria Teresa, (Tere), who had married an English naval officer. Nicholas Dolan was stationed in Portsmouth at that time, and Margarita stayed with them. The earliest photograph I have of her was taken before we met, (Photos No. 1). It was there that she was first introduced to Ian. Perhaps he had met the Dolans through the Spanish Embassy. Ian spoke perfect Spanish, and he was an obvious partner for Margarita at the dinners and dances that were part of life in the Navy. She was supposed to be learning English, but in that circle of family and friends, it is doubtful she practiced much.

But not long after Margarita's arrival, Lt. Comm. Dolan was sent to Singapore, and his family retreated to Tere's mother's home in Cadiz, in the south-west of Spain. But Margarita was not ready to return home. She became an *au pair* to a family living in Southsea. She was poorly paid and, apart from looking after two young children, was expected to clean the house, as well as other household chores; slave labour, you would correctly call it! She lasted a month there. One day, she took off, telling the woman of the house that she could no longer stand it. As she left, the little girl of the house caught her finger in the door, (not Margarita's fault), but she always said she was glad that she was not there alone with the child, to take the blame for that incident.

Her cousin having gone, Margarita had only one contact, so she headed to London to find Ian in No.2, Church Crescent, Muswell Hill. She secured a job in the Nurses' Home attached to Hampstead General Hospital, and she and Ian went out together. Ian had found the girl of his dreams, and even told his parents that he was going to marry her. As for her, she had no such ideas! In fact, Margarita told me later that she and Ian never held hands, and that he was cold to the point that she had some hidden mistrust of him. He would sometimes sing romantic songs to the accompaniment of his guitar, and it would turn her off completely!

So, on that morning in early June, I sat down at the table with Margarita, completely unaware of what was about to happen. At our meeting in the Wagon & Horses, we had felt no particular attraction for each other. In fact, Margarita later told me that she thought John was the more handsome; true perhaps. But on pouring over the exercise book, our arms accidentally touched, and a strong sensation passed through me. I know she felt it too. Our eyes met and, a few seconds later, our lips came together. Wham! I was in a daze. It was as if I was suffocating. We could no longer stay in that room together. What if Ian were to arrive? He would immediately know that something was up! As we were leaving the house, disorientated and not knowing where we would go, Ian drove up in his Mini van to meet her and saw us together. He became wildly jealous and violently angry. He took hold of Margarita and pushed her into the passenger seat of his Mini, leaving me standing at the gate, upset and bewildered. He told her that she should never see me again, and drove off to Hampstead. He said that if she were not for him, she was not for me either. But love has no barriers, and Margarita and I had already fallen in love at that table in the front room of the flat.

Later, Margarita told me that Ian had already painted an unfavourable picture of me; that I always left the kitchen in a mess, among other things. Me! dirty? Could he have had an uncomfortable feeling in the back of his mind that I was in some way a threat to their relationship? I think not, and I had never given him any reason to think so.

John, Ian and I had arranged to go sailing to the Channel Islands that very weekend, and therefore it was well over a week before Margarita and I met again. Cooped up on a yacht in the English Channel, after what had happened, was a strain. Ian and I never spoke a word to each other that week. Fortunately, there was Mike Crabtree and two more experienced sailors, making a party of six.

I had done some dinghy sailing in the Persian Gulf, but the English Channel was an entirely different kettle of fish. The Channel Islands have some of the highest tides in the world, as well as unpredictable winds and weather. However, we were young and adventure was in the blood. I began the week with naïve confidence. I cannot remember what we had agreed in advance, but I had bought a book on navigation, and had swatted up in the days before our departure from the coast of Devon. I studied theoretically the art of navigation, using a compass, and plotting a course on a chart, considering the effects of wind strength, direction and the effect of tides.

We sailed out of Salcombe harbour on a fine and breezy afternoon, and headed south. The two experienced crew members handled the two-masted ketch, assisted by John and Ian, while Mike and I sat below deck, plotting our course towards St. Peter Port, the main town of the island of Guernsey. We sailed all night, and early in the morning, the coast of Guernsey came into sight. We sailed straight into St. Peter Port harbour. I was pleased that my newly acquired navigation skills, as well as Mike's mathematical genius, had contributed to a direct hit!

After some hours in harbour, we decided to sail to the island of Sark, a tiny island part of the Channel Islands. Sark had an element of self-government under the hereditary Dame of Sark, and with a population of under six hundred souls. But we were unaware that the harbour was only accessible at high tide. We discovered this on approaching the entrance in the evening at low tide, and we had no choice but to turn around, and make our way back to St. Peter Port, or another harbour. It was an extremely anxious time. The night seemed interminable. The tide was racing, there was not much wind, and we could see the rocky coastline just a short way away. We were strangers in very unfriendly territory, sailing up and down, and I for one was very scared. I expected at any moment to strike a dark rock. Would I ever see my new-found love again? However, morning came and we were able to see our way back to St. Peter Port. It was a relief to be back in harbour.

After a week of smooth sailing, it was time to return to England's shores. The navigation back to Salcombe was as successful as on the outward journey. We entered the harbour, hardly having to alter course at all. I for one was happy to be back on dry land. It had been an adventurous week, with its moments of elation, as well as its moments of terror.

Back in Upper Basildon, my thoughts immediately turned to Margarita, whom I had met the week before, but had immediately lost. Would I find her? Would our feelings be the same? Would she even want to see me? You could forgive me for having these doubts. After all, our meeting and parting had occurred within an hour. It was almost as if it had been a dream. So, it was with some trepidation that I returned to London. I could not count on Ian for any help: we were not on speaking terms. But my doubts were dispelled, when I drove up to Hampstead General Hospital and found her waiting for me. She was dressed in a brown uniform, of which she was ashamed. To me, it didn't matter in the least. I was overwhelmed with joy at seeing her: the uniform was of no consequence whatsoever.

I knew that I could no longer stay in that flat with Ian, so I found a bed-sitter in a road just off Muswell Hill Road, nearer to Highgate tube station than Church Crescent. I came across Ian in the year that followed, until I left Thomson McLintock's London Office and moved to Bath in Somerset. We may have passed the time of day, but no more. He kept in touch with Margarita's cousin, Tere and her husband, Nicholas, and from them we knew that he later married an English girl and had children, living for a time in New Zealand, and then in Holland. He never managed to qualify as a Chartered Accountant. We also knew that he suffered an attack of aneurism and passed away in his late fifties. Did he ever secretly wish he had married Margarita? And did he harbour a grudge against me until later in his life? I do not know, but I never wished him any harm, and in a way, I owe him a great debt of gratitude, since it was through him that I met my partner of forty-six years. It is interesting that, according to Tere, Ian's widow closely resembled Margarita. He must have had a very clear idea what his perfect partner should look like!

Margarita enjoyed her job at the Nurses' Home, despite its domestic nature. As a non-citizen, that kind of work was the only kind she was allowed to do. The lady in charge was kind and motherly, as well as being a prodigious tea-drinker. Margarita counted thirteen cups one day! She was busy supplying the lady's enormous caffeine needs, making the nurses' beds and cleaning. Every evening, we would go out together, enjoying the long summer evenings. One of our favourite haunts was The Flask, a pretty pub in Highgate. We sat over half-pints of beer, holding hands and just revelling in being together. Ian had taken her to many expensive restaurants, and we often joked about the come-down to half-pints! But being together was what mattered. It hardly mattered that her English was still very basic, and my Spanish totally non-existent: we were on the same wavelength.

During that summer, Beatlemania was still going strong, but the records that became a kind of signature tune for us were 'Monday, Monday' and

'California Dreamin' by The Mammas and the Papas. California was the centre of all that was new and progressive in the Western World. Even now, the West Coast is the home of most of the spiritually enlightened proponents of New Age Thought. Recently, it became the first of the fifty states to ban three additives commonly used in bread and other foods in the USA, but banned for years by many developed countries of the world.

During my trip to England in the spring of 1995, I read through my mother's diary for the year 1966, noting the various references to Margarita's visits to Upper Basildon. Sadly, those diaries no longer exist; wrongly destroyed without the permission of my brother, John or me. But I know that very soon after returning from the sailing holiday, I took her down to Green Harbour to introduce her to Mum. I have a slide that I took of Margarita in front of the house that weekend. Country life was something new for her, having been raised in a town. Our family loved long walks in the country. It took Margarita some time to appreciate the enjoyment of walking through woods and across fields, without shop windows to gaze into. I was also brought up in a concrete jungle, but our holidays were spent in the countryside, and we grew to love the beauty of our natural world.

I think my mother was surprised that I should have fallen for a girl from beyond our shores. Mum was English through and through, and she could not have entertained the possibility of living permanently abroad. Her eleven years in Kuwait were for her a time in limbo, without her children near, as well as her parents and sisters, with whom she had always been close. She made the most of her time out there in the heat, and she and Dad did things they would never have done in England. But throughout that time, she was looking forward to the next holiday. It was only when she and Dad returned to England that she came into her own. Ironically, both John and I were to marry foreigners, leaving England to live overseas, so, sadly for her, she was not to have her two sons for long.

There were moments during that first weekend in Upper Basildon that I cannot forget, like the excitement of taking Margarita a cup of tea in bed on the first morning. Green Harbour was a bungalow, but Dad had had the roof space converted into a bedroom for John and me. Margarita slept in the single room downstairs.

The 30th July 1966 was a great day for English football. We had gone camping that weekend to our favourite spot by the river Lyd, on the edge of Dartmoor. Mum, John, Jean, Margarita and I huddled inside a small tent, while the cold rain fell outside. We listened on a transistor radio to that tense World Cup final in Wembley Stadium, in which England beat Germany 4-2. Playing for England in that match, under the guidance of manager Alf Ramsey, were great players like Captain Bobby Moore, Martin Peters and Geoff Hurst, the striker who scored two goals in extra time to clinch victory for England. It was England's first World Cup victory and, sad to say, England has not won the Cup in the fifty-odd years since then. England, the home of football, has produced many talented players, but seems not to be able to produce results at the international level. English tennis has not fared better. Since the Open Era began in 1968, only three male players and two female players have won a title to date. Of these, only Andy Murray and Virginia Wade can truly be recognised as world class. One wonders what is lacking in the English make-up!

At the end of one weekend spent at Green Harbour, Margarita and I drove back to London late on the Sunday evening. We had driven as far as Reading, when the fan belt of the Mini broke, causing the water in the radiator to boil. We decided to press on, stopping periodically to fill up with cold water, and allowing the engine to cool. It was a long journey, but we finally reached the house where Margarita was staying at 4 am. Not wanting to alert the inmates of her arrival at that ungodly hour, she managed to creep through a downstairs window. I was due to start an audit in Lincolnshire that morning, and had to face a long drive, not having had any sleep. I almost nodded off several times, and finally had to pull off the road and sleep for a while. I do not recall, but I must have had a new fan belt fitted before leaving for Lincolnshire.

That reminds me of a frightening incident that happened to us one evening. We had decided to stop somewhere quiet, and have a peaceful cuddle. So, we drove into a car park on the edge of Hampstead Heath, and sat talking in the back seat. It was already dark, and the huge car park was completely deserted. Just then, I saw the headlights of a car approaching from behind. Despite the available space, the car drew up alongside ours, and the driver extinguished the car lights. The motive of the driver could not have been anything but sinister. Then another car appeared, and was making its way towards us. I scrambled into the front seat, heart thumping, and started the engine. I quickly backed out. With shaking hands, I drove out of that car park as fast as I could. Whatever they intended, we managed to escape, with tremendous relief!

Those few weeks were idyllic, but like all good times, they had to come to an end. Margarita's father got to hear and fear that his only daughter was loose in London, and ordered her back to Spain without delay. One fine evening, we went for a drink at The Old Bull and Bush, a well-known pub on the way to Golders Green, the affluent Jewish suburb of North London. Sitting outside, we mourned the fact that our time together was rapidly coming to an end, but plans were made to meet again as soon as possible.

And it was not long before we *did* meet again, this time on her own home ground. I had some leave due to me, so I persuaded my brother to accompany me on an adventure to Spain; a country in Europe that I had never visited. I had only been to Switzerland and Paris. Now Spain was beckoning. It was to be the first of many holidays spent in that country.

We took the car across the English Channel by way of the Newhaven/Dieppe ferry, which docked early one morning in early September. Driving south through Normandy, along the straight and narrow, tree-lined road, I could feel the very heart of France; the sleepy little villages, where I could imagine cheese was made at home. As our maroon Mini sped south, we felt the increasing warmth of late summer. We drove through Poitiers, and on down towards the wine growing region of Bordeaux. In the late afternoon, we pulled off the road and pitched our little orange tent in a field. We dared not light a fire, because we were on private land. We slept right away, rising early the next morning, without anyone discovering our presence.

The second day on the road brought us through the heavily scented pine forests of the Bordeaux region, and on to the border with Spain at Hendaya. In the afternoon we were motoring west towards Bilbao, the industrial capital of the Basque country. Northern Spain in those days was devoid of motorways, and main roads were narrow and badly maintained, winding up mountains and precariously down through valleys. There was little motor traffic, but plenty of wooden oxcarts, loaded with hay or other farm produce, creaking along as they had done for generations. Passing them was difficult on such winding roads, and progress was slow. The second night stop was taken in similar fashion, in a field by the side of the road. We had not covered the distance we had hoped, and were left with a long and tiring drive for the third and final day.

Asturias is a mountainous region, and the roads were no better than those of the Basque country. But I was determined to reach La Coruna by nightfall, even though we had not notified anyone of our impending arrival. The car behaved beautifully, and finally, at about six o'clock in the evening, we drove down the long hill, with the city ahead of us. Excitement was mounting! But what reception would we get from her family, and from Margarita herself? And more immediately, would we find the house? Driving into the centre of the city, I asked a *guardia civil,* who was directing the traffic at *El Obelisco,* for *Calle* San Andres. At that point, we were at the end of that very street. We found No. 6-8, climbed to the first floor and rang the bell. I forget who opened for us. It was not Margarita. Anyway, we were taken by someone to the flat of Marcial, her father's cousin, where we were to stay. It was not considered the done thing for Margarita and I to stay in the same house. Marcial, much younger than his cousin, was a Captain in the Spanish Army, and also a Chemist. He lived next to the Army barracks, a short walk from San Andres. One thing I remember about him was his curious habit of making ice of different colours. Margarita came there as soon as she heard of our arrival. I will never forget how we opened the door, and she burst in, flinging her arms around me. She was delighted, and you can imagine how *I* felt!

Spain in the 1960's was firmly under the authority of *Generalissimo* Franco, the dictator who had defeated the Republicans in the bitter civil war of 1936 to 1939. Spain was backward, economically undeveloped, and outside the recently established European Common Market. A rigid class system consisted of the political elite, a small affluent middle class and a huge peasantry. There was little socialising between classes. In a town of about a quarter of a million people, Margarita's father, Dr. Pio Garcia Lopez, the dermatologist, was well-known in middle class circles. In that class it was important what people wore in the street, who their friends were and which schools the children attended. The effects of the beat generation, which was already well established in Britain, had yet to be felt. Everyone was expected to conform to the social rules. Boys wore their hair short, and the dress code, especially for girls, was strict. Margarita had bought a purple suit in England, the skirt of which showed her knees. Her family refused to allow her to walk in the street dressed that way. Into that setting appeared two young men with longish, Beatle-style hair and boots with pointed toes; adeptly called 'winkle-pickers.' Everywhere John and I went, people stared. I believe Margarita's family was unnerved by our appearance. She herself cared little what people thought, and I think she must have felt excitement that we were the subject of so much interest. In fact, she considered those who stared at us to be *paletos,* the Spanish word for peasants.

Margarita had lost her mother in 1961, and Don Pio had married a woman of about forty years from Cordoba in Andalucia. The union was one of convenience: he was the dominant partner, and this is just how he wanted it. As a handsome widower in his fifties, he had been propositioned by a wealthy woman from Madrid, but he would have none of it!

Margarita and her stepmother did not get on. Lolita was an intruder in the eyes of her stepdaughter, and to Lolita, Margarita was a rebellious and troublesome teenager. But father and daughter were very close, much to Lolita's chagrin. She laid down rules of behaviour for Margarita and me, ensuring that we were never alone together, and insisting on a chaperone whenever we went out together. But we did not mind: we could not leave John behind. Margarita had a close friend, Maribel, and the four of us often went to the beach together. John and I stayed for about ten days in La Coruna, but before leaving, Margarita and I pledged ourselves to each other.

One of our favourite beaches was by the village of Mera, across the bay from La Coruna. It was there, sitting on a rock overlooking the sea, that I proposed marriage. She was surprised, because I had told her before, jokingly, that I did not want to get married. However, she said a firm 'yes' to my proposal. The moment we arrived back home, she dashed into her father's surgery to tell him the news. Margarita was never one to let the grass grow under her feet! Her father must have been deeply concerned at the news, having never considered the possibility that she would marry a foreigner. But he judged that, once I had returned to England, she would soon forget me. He found her a job in a bank and nothing more was said.

But we wrote letters to each other regularly. There is an adorable photograph of her, on the back of which she wrote, 'I love you', with her signature, (Photo No. 2). It is unclear at which time it was taken. My heart aches whenever I see this photo now! We did not forget each other, as her father had hoped. We agreed that she would come to England at Christmas, and this she shared with her father. He merely said that she could go if she paid for her ticket herself, believing that this could not happen. They said no more about it, but she saved the money, and the day before she was due to leave for England, she told him she was going the next day. What could he say? He had already given his permission! But he was shocked nonetheless.

Meanwhile, life in my bed-sitter was peaceful. I cooked for myself and did my own laundry. I began to expand my horizons, reading books on philosophy, and contemplating the nature of God and my place in the Universe. The nihilist philosophy of Jean-Paul Sartre gripped me for some time, but I eventually rejected it as morbid. My experience of Christianity had given me no satisfaction. But it was to be many years before I was to be confronted by Eastern spiritual philosophy, by which time New Age ideas were becoming widespread.

Margarita duly arrived in London for a short stay. She took a room in Belsize Park, in a boarding house run by a Mrs. Mendelssohn, having promised her father that she would not stay in my room. We honoured that promise. It was December, and she was not used to the English winter. She had to feed the meter with shillings in order to have some warmth in her room, and at night she would pile onto her bed everything she could find, even her suitcase! She had come to London in the company of Ricardo, a young man from La Coruna. He stayed in the same house, but without payment, because he kept the landlady warm at night in return for bed and board!

My father had retired from Kuwait Oil Company at the end of that summer, and he and Mum were staying at Green Harbour, while they were looking for their dream cottage. Margarita and I spent Christmas with them. John, who had returned from a spell of working with a famous Architect in Chicago, was there. He had brought with him a set of three LP records of Billie Holiday, the American Jazz singer. Those records were played many times in the ensuing years, and remain among my favourite music. The LPs are no longer playable, but easily available at the tap of the screen. Jean was also at home. Margarita's English was still not fluent and she missed much of the conversation. Much of the humour passed her by. It is uncomfortable not being able to laugh along with the others. It was therefore hard for her to feel part of the family.

She returned to England again at Easter, by which time my parents had bought Yew Cottage, a three-hundred-year-old pair of semi-detached cottages, with a substantial garden and a large field, backing into beech woods. It was a short walk down Bethesda Street from Green Harbour. John employed his architectural skills, converting the two dwellings into a comfortable home with four bedrooms. He and Dad spent weeks working happily together, knocking down walls, constructing a single, central staircase and redecorating. Mum and Dad bought a grey mare and named her Beth. I remember a slide of Margarita riding Beth in the field during that holiday.

Margarita and I decided to get married in England, because Spanish law only provided for marriage in the Catholic Church. I was not prepared to swear that our children would be brought up in the Catholic faith, which I would not do. It was only after the death of General Franco in 1976, when the monarchy was restored and democracy was established, that our union was recognised there.

Margarita's father had a close friend in the Spanish army, who had been the Military Attaché in London. Don Pio asked his military friend to investigate the Hawley family's circumstances; my father's profession, position in society, income and so on. In Spain at that time it was possible to do that, the middle class being small enough to ensure that someone living in the same town could easily find out about the one under investigation. In England such an idea was comical. So why not invite the whole of Chris' family to Spain to meet their in-laws? And so it was arranged. My parents, brother and sister were to accompany me, to be scrutinised by Don Pio. I am not clear about my parents' first reactions to the idea, but we made the trip by car in July 1967, following the same route that John and I had used the year before; this time in the comfort of the Wolseley.

Imagine the scene! My family spoke no Spanish and Margarita's family no English. Margarita was not trusted to be the interpreter: Don Pio wanted a translator one-hundred-percent trustworthy. Jesus, the Military Attaché, was called in again. I was not concerned with what they discussed, but I know that they got on well. The marriage received Don Pio's blessing, having received the assurance that his daughter was marrying into a good family. In the meantime, the betrothed ones had a good time. We became impatient to know each other better, and one day, we declared we were going to the beach. Instead, we made for the room that had been rented for me in *La Calle Real* nearby. After all, we would be married in just one month. To fool the folks, we wetted our swimming costumes, but we didn't fool Carmen, the family servant! She was sharp! She tasted the costumes, and found no salt. She confronted us, and we told her the truth. She was good enough to say nothing to anyone else, fortunately!

We took my family on some car trips around Galicia. It was my parents' first experience of Spain, but not the last. Two events stuck in my memory; the first because of its anxiety, and the second because of its charm. We were camping, apparently in a place we should not have been, and we were accosted by two policemen. Margarita kept quiet, and we declared complete ignorance of the crime, and the Spanish language. The policemen decided to forget it. The second event was memorable. We stopped for lunch one day at a tiny rural café. The owner told us that his wife was not available, but we could prepare our own. So, Margarita cooked *una tortilla* (Spanish omelette) in their kitchen, and we enjoyed it with crusty Spanish bread and a bottle of the local wine. For an English family, it was an amazing experience, one that our own country could never have offered.

The wedding was fixed for the ninth day of the ninth month. In later years, we came to know the special power of the number nine, but in 1967 we were unfamiliar with sacred numerology. My parents had already discussed the ceremony with the vicar in Upper Basildon, in view of the fact that Margarita was a Catholic. But in that respect, the Anglican Church took a liberal position, and the vicar had no problem marrying us. The bans were read on three consecutive Sundays, as is the custom.

After the holiday, the whole family drove back to England, leaving me behind to enjoy another two weeks in Galicia, chaperone-free. I had left Thomson McLintock in June 1967, having taken my final examinations. I was now free to enjoy an extended holiday, hoping that the examiners would be pleased with my answers and would accord me a pass. It happened that way, for which I was very relieved. Studying again for a repeat attempt once married did not appeal to me one bit!

So, I remained in Spain, while Mum and Dad prepared for the wedding. We had already put in an order for the wedding invitations in English, (Photo No.3). In Spain, we had one printed in Spanish. Towards the end of August, I returned home by ship from Vigo, the second port of Galicia. On board the ship, I met a small group of young people my own age, and had a last fling with a pretty Welsh girl, who knew I was about to be wed. There was no attachment involved, and nothing more than a kiss or two was shared.

Wisely, my parents were not in favour of expensive wedding parties. Mum made the cake and prepared all the food, as she later did for both John's and Jean's wedding breakfasts. The church ceremony was held at the pretty, medieval Lower Basildon Church, in sight of the River Thames, as it winds its way through the Goring Gap between the Chiltern Hills and the Berkshire Downs.

Margarita's brother, Jose Luis, was sent to give away the bride, her father being unwilling to make the journey. Lolita also attended the wedding, as well as one of Margarita's cousins from Andalucia. Lolita made a completely unnecessary fuss the evening before the wedding, when she discovered Margarita and I alone in the sitting room, merely talking! Jose Luis was a lawyer and a budding politician. Another attribute I discovered that night was his gift for stentorian snoring. Jose's vibrations rocked the house. It was particularly sleep threatening for me, sleeping on the other side of the wall from him. I often wondered how his wife tolerated it year after year!

Margarita told me later, that in the morning of our wedding day, she had second thoughts about the marriage, and voiced her doubts to her brother. In Photo No. 4, they are seen approaching the church. He said she had to go through with it, since he had come all the way to England for that purpose. In truth, she found it hard to adapt to English ways, and on returning from honeymoon, and staying in my parents' house, she *did* have serious doubts that she had done the right thing by marrying an English boy. It was one of the reasons why, three years later, we decided to live in a neutral country. She was not the only one who felt out of place. I experienced similar reactions when in her home environment. On one occasion, I was close to tears. Living in an independent country gave us both a freedom to express ourselves, without the restraints of our two cultures.

The wedding and the reception at Yew Cottage went off smoothly, thanks to a fine and warm late summer day. Photo No. 5 shows the newly-wedded couple coming out of the church. Photos Nos. 6, 7 and 8 show family groups. My family was well represented at the wedding. Of my grandparents, only my father's father was missing, having passed away in 1963. In Photo No. 9, Nanna and Grandad Walker pose with my cousin, Marion and family, at the reception in Yew Cottage. Uncle Dennis, always the schemer, laced the bride's drink with a mixture of spirits, which made her vomit out of the car window after we had set off on honeymoon, all but ruining our first night!

In the late afternoon, the wedding party saw off the Mini, to the back bumper of which had been tied numerous pots and pans. These were to come in useful, as I shall relate later. We had to stop to remove coins from inside the wheel hubs, as well as allowing the bride some fresh air. We planned to spend our honeymoon camping in Ireland, but I had decided to book a night at The Queen's Hotel in Cheltenham, a couple of hours drive from Upper Basildon. It was an old-fashioned hotel, with roots in the prosperous Regency days, when the wealthy came to the Spa to take the waters. Our room had no bathroom of its own. I cannot imagine how it earned its five stars!

We took the ferry from Fishguard in Wales to Rosslaire in County Wicklow. Wicklow is a hilly, sparsely populated county in the extreme south-east of Eire, south of the capital, Dublin, and it was ideal for camping. We found several lovely level and grassy spots by sparkling clean rivers. The weather was kind to us, allowing us to keep a wood fire, on which we cooked. We had only a small, two-man tent, so the fine weather was appreciated. One night, I awoke with a dread that I might lose my new-found happiness, due to the volatile Middle East situation, following Israel's recent victory in the Six Day War against Egypt, Jordan, Syria and Iraq. Many people saw the danger of the conflict escalating into an international affair. I was not yet twenty-six, and I might have been called up, had Britain gone to war. Perhaps my dread was irrational, but I had embarked on a life with the girl of my dreams, and any threat to that was hard to contemplate.

The pots and pans that we had untied from the car came in useful several days into our holiday. We had camped beside a stream. Too lazy to wash our dishes before going to bed, we left them all outside, intending to do it in the morning. It rained heavily that night. When we crawled out of the tent the following morning, the stream had become a raging torrent, and all our dirty dishes and pots had been washed away. For the remainder of the holiday, we were forced to fall back on the dented specimens that we were glad we had not thrown away. But the next night, we retreated to the shelter of a modest guest house to escape a bout of rainy weather.

After visiting the ancient Capital City of Dublin, we headed north into the province of my birth. We walked down Agincourt Avenue in Belfast, and I pointed out to Margarita the attic room in which I had been born. We took the car ferry over to Stranraer, in Scotland, where we called on Dad's relations; Auntie Daisy and her son and family, before pointing the nose of the faithful Mini southwards.

MARRIED LIFE

BACK IN YEW COTTAGE, I had to turn my attention to settling into a place of our own, and finding a job. I had given in my notice to TMcL, London immediately after sitting for the Part V examination in June. After seven years in the London office, I needed a change. It was now September. Returning from honeymoon, during which all future concerns had been temporarily forgotten, I knew that we had no time to waste. Margarita was uncomfortable staying with my family. Predictably, it was the mother-in-law, daughter-in-law relationship that was the bone of contention. Mum was not the easiest person to live with for a daughter-in-law, who had usurped the position of caring for the eldest son. John's wife, Cathy encountered the same feeling, when they married in 1972.

Within one month, I had secured a job in the Bristol office of Thomson McLintock & Co., and Margarita and I drove down to the West Country to find a place to live. We chose the beautiful City of Bath, about twelve miles from Bristol on the A4 from London. Bath, like Cheltenham, was a fashionable Spa town in the 18th Century. It is built almost entirely of yellow stone, and many of its more beautiful housing developments are from that period. But Bath's history goes back to before Roman times. Sulis was a Celtic goddess, worshipped by the inhabitants of the settlement that occupied the site on which the modern City stands. Aquae Sulis, (the waters of Sulis), was the name given to the City by the Romans. The only natural hot springs in the whole of Britain were channelled into baths there. After the fall of the

Roman Empire, the baths were buried and forgotten by the unwashed natives of the land, until they were rediscovered in the Victorian era, and renovated. With their love for the ornate, the Victorians embellished the simple baths with extravagant structures and neo-Roman columns. During the celebrations in 1973 to mark the one thousandth anniversary of the crowning of Edgar, the first King of all England, in Bath Abbey, the baths were opened to the public, and we had the rare privilege of swimming in them. Where the heavily mineralised water issues from the ground, the bath is hot, (caldarium). The water flows into another cooler bath, (tepidarium), and then into the final bath, (frigidarium), by which time the water is cold. The last bath is rectangular and surrounded by a flat expanse of flagstones, worn down by many sandaled Roman feet. Apart from the Victorian extravaganza above, one can revel in the Roman grace and charm at ground level, and imagine one is in the company of a superior race, elegantly-dressed in white togas and flowing robes.

A little-known event, which took place in Victorian Bath in 1864, was the sudden death of one of the great African explorers. John Hanning Speke had travelled, together with Richard Francis Burton, across East Africa, from the coast to Lake Victoria in search of the source of the River Nile. The two characters were poles apart. Burton was a brilliant scholar, who could speak seven languages. In contrast, Speke was a brave, headstrong young man. He was convinced that the falls he found was the source of the White Nile. The careful, and perhaps jealous Burton, who had not accompanied Speke all the way to the falls, said there was no evidence, and accused Speke of glory hunting. A conference was arranged in the Pump Room in Bath by the Royal Geographical Society. Both Burton and Speke were due to give an address, each putting forward his own argument for and against the Source of the Nile claim. The meeting promised to be a fiery one. The delegates were kept waiting for the arrival of Speke, who had gone hunting in the morning on his estate near Box. Finally, it was announced that he had died of gunshot wounds. Apparently, the gun had gone off accidentally, as he was climbing over a stone wall. Was it accidental, or had he committed suicide? Had he got cold feet at the prospect of facing his travelling companion, the scholar and orator? Speke's death remains a mystery. However, later expeditions to the source of the Nile confirmed that Speke was correct.

We found a top-floor furnished flat in a Georgian terrace in Duke Street, a pedestrian street a stone's throw from the Abbey. Our window overlooked the River Avon, where swans glided peacefully by. Beyond, lay the County Cricket ground, where Somerset sometimes played, and further off, behind a residential area, rose green hills to the south-east. Actually, the flat was a poor attempt at carving out the necessary rooms from a small attic. The kitchen and living room were created from a reasonably sized room, by means of a simple partition that cut the only window in two, and resulted in a very narrow, cramped living room and an even narrower, cramped kitchen. The bathtub took up almost the entire space of the bathroom, which occupied a part of the landing. But to us it was a cosy home, away from family, in which we could do what we liked, how we liked and when we liked. We moved there in late October, and I started working again. Margarita found a job in a chemist's shop in Poultney Road, just across the bridge.

Living in the centre of that lovely town of just over eighty-thousand people was a wonderful experience. We used to walk the streets and river footpaths, admiring the elegant architecture and fashionable shops. We opened an account at Barclays Bank in Milsom Street, and often spent our Saturday mornings shopping, when we were not visiting my parents at the weekend. One of my strongest memories is the regular visits to the little crowded café on beautiful 18th Century Poultney Bridge, where they served excellent coffee and hamburgers rich in tasty onions. I can smell and taste them now! We liked to walk around the Circus, a beautiful ring of Georgian residences, with a circular garden in the middle and along the fine and stately Royal Crescent. I used to wish we could have afforded to buy a flat there, with a spectacular view over the City.

One of our first evening excursions was to dine at one of Bath's expensive restaurants; The Hole in the Wall. Margarita and I both chose a rabbit casserole, which was delicious but very rich. My stomach coped better than hers. By the time we had reached Duke Street, her rabbit had been left behind!

We bought a very expensive white German dinner and tea service (Thomas) in Domus 7, a little shop in a cute arcade in the City centre. We thought we were being a touch extravagant, but remnants of this collection were still in use decades later! A very attractive ornamental plate, given to us as a wedding present, was to take pride of place on the wall of the stairs, facing the front door. But as I was fixing it to the wall, it fell and broke into pieces. I was terrified that my new wife would shout at me, and I hesitated to break the news to her. But how could I hide it? In the end, she did forgive me! But I was not the only one to ask forgiveness. One day, she made a meal in a Pyrex dish, but before we could taste it, the dish was transformed into thousands of pieces on the kitchen floor.

Our bedroom was painted beige and green. Sunday was the day for a lie-in, listening to the sound of the church bells from a nearby steeple. We never stepped into that church, but the sound of the bells was our Sunday morning music. Margarita was disinterested in searching for a Catholic Church.

Following in my father's footsteps, I experimented with beer and wine making. One particularly successful wine came from rhubarb. I bottled it, thinking that it had finished fermenting, only to realise that it was still working in the bottle. It turned out to be a very dry and fruity sparkling wine. One bottle exploded in the cupboard, where it had been stored: you can imagine the mess...and the smell! One autumn, I was given a load of ripe pears, and I proceeded to make perry in the bathtub. I thank my long-suffering wife for her patience! I had a stock of those old-fashioned screw-top bottles. Sadly, they have long been replaced by the bane of the modern world; plastic, or thin glass bottles with flimsy metal or plastic tops.

We had few friends in Bath, but we befriended one young couple. Ian delivered milk in his home area. They lived in the village of Core, near Box, on the hills on the London side of Bath. His wife, Cathy worked with Margarita in her second job at Paris Fashion Wigs, where the two girls removed the labels, 'Made in Japan' with others that read, 'Real European Hair.' So much for human values in commerce! I was Ian's best man at their wedding, at which a famous comedian, whose name I forget, also gave a talk. We were good friends with Ian and Cathy and enjoyed their company but, as so often happens, we lost contact with them once we moved from the flat.

Our neighbours in the flat below owned a butcher's shop in the town. They were much older than we were. I do not recall their names: we just referred to them as 'the butchers'. They were heavy smokers, and early in the morning, we could hear the unpleasant sound of violent coughing. But that was not the only thing that disturbed us. Mrs Butcher told Margarita that her husband's favourite dish was jugged hare, which entails hanging the little beast for a week of two, until it is crawling with maggots. They were people who were not in favour of opening windows, so that their flat permanently smelt of stale food. It quite put us off! Margarita remembered that they were members of a social club in Bath, and they took us there once, but we disliked the atmosphere.

Some weekends, we drove to Upper Basildon, to stay with my parents, who were now well established in Yew Cottage. During the years that followed, they developed a small market garden, kept chickens and ducks, and later, high yielding goats as well. My father had a delivery round in the neighbourhood, and as far as Pangbourne, selling to his regular customers organic produce and goat's milk. In the beginning, surplus hens and ducks might end up in the pot, but as time went on, Dad got attached to the feathered creatures, and even gave them names. You can imagine how he felt about wringing their little necks! There is no way you can bite on the leg of Daphne Duck and feel good! So, the lucky creatures were allowed to live out their retirement in peace. Eventually, Mum and Dad opened their cottage to paying guests during the summer months, and converted the roomy garden shed into a cosy bedroom for themselves. Always busy, they enjoyed working together. I believe the days in Yew Cottage were the happiest of their lives.

We became familiar with the different mushrooms and fungi while staying at Yew Cottage. We collected some varieties from the fields, but also in the woods. As children, we had been told not to pick mushrooms found beneath trees, because field mushrooms, just about the only kind eaten by the English at that time, do not grow under trees. Wood Blewits and Parasol mushrooms are two of the species we liked, and we often brought them home from our early morning walks and cooked them for breakfast. In fact, of all the varieties indigenous to England, very few are actually poisonous. Nature has given deadly species bright colours, to warn would-be predators, 'Hey, I'm poisonous', they are saying! Later, when we had moved from the centre of Bath to Lower Weston, we picked shaggy caps, also known as Lawyer's Wigs, in the recreation ground, and made soup. One year, we were amazed at the profusion of the tall, spindly fruit bodies that one morning just appeared.

Although I was happy living in Bath, my job was the least satisfying of my working life. The firm had recently taken over the local firm of Grace, Derbyshire & Todd, and it occupied one large room in the British Aircraft Corporation offices at Filton, north of Bristol. BAC was the main client of our Bristol office. The Manager was a Mr. Pickard, an uninspiring middle-aged man, who managed a staff of about six. The BAC audit was deadly boring, and when the boss was not in the office, we used to spend hours gossiping. Most of the members of staff were middle aged, and not interested in 'going anywhere'. Tony Seal, although still young, declared that he was an armchair traveller, meaning he would rather see the world on the television from the comfort of his armchair. Not for me that life! Mr. Huckstable, or 'Huck' as we called him, was quite a character; fat and jolly. I learnt later that he ended his days under a motor vehicle while crossing the road. Jess was the comptometer operator; a kindly, middle-aged mother who was fond of chatting.

Robin Wilkinson, by far the most serious and educated of the bunch, lived in a charming, Georgian terraced house in the salubrious suburb of Clifton, close to the Clifton Suspension Bridge. Margarita and I went to dinner with Robin and his family one evening.

The famous bridge was built by one of the boldest and most flamboyant figures of Victorian England. Isambard Kingdom Brunel was the son of a French civil engineer and was born in 1806. He became famous for his iron ships that transformed international shipping, in particular the seventy-six metre *Great Western,* the longest ship of its time, which narrowly missed being the first steam-driven ship to cross the Atlantic. Later, the much larger *Great Eastern* was designed to carry four-thousand passengers from England to Australia. He was the first to use the propeller instead of the paddle. He was also the builder of the Thames Tunnel and the designer of Paddington Station in London, as well as various other bridges, dockyards and railway stations throughout the country. The importance of Swindon as a railway centre is largely due to Brunel. But he was not without critics. There were strong objections to his Clifton Bridge, began in 1831. Civil Engineers of the day, notably the influential Thomas Telford, doubted the advisability of putting a two-hundred-and-fourteen metre span over a gorge that was seventy-six metres deep. In the event, construction was halted due to lack of funds, and the bridge was not completed until 1864, five years after Brunel's death. But Brunel's ingenious and tasteful design has stood the test of time, and today, one-hundred-and-sixty years after completion, it is as solid as the day it was opened. More than four-million vehicles cross it every year!

One memorable day at Filton was the day that Captain Brian Trubshaw took up the supersonic Concorde for its maiden flight. Concorde was a joint project with the French National plane maker. It was a flag waving attempt on the part of the British and the French to beat the Americans at supersonic passenger travel. It cost millions of pounds, and failed to pave the way for universal supersonic air travel. I believe only the USSR attempted to compete with Concorde with its unsuccessful Tupolev, which actually beat Concorde to the skies. The world went straight back to subsonic passenger travel, and supersonic aircraft has still not made a comeback. The Concorde was not cost effective, and metal fatigue-related accidents put the lid on further development. But I felt grateful for the opportunity to witness the maiden flight!

During my stay with TMcL Bristol, the firm moved to offices near the City centre. The firm were the auditors of a large national bakery group, and one of the more interesting audits was the Bristol subsidiary that operated a factory in a southern suburb of the City. It was one of the first large audits for which I was the senior in charge. I chiefly remember it because it was at this time that the sectarian violence flared up in Northern Ireland.

My 'finest hour' in Bristol came shortly before leaving the firm. I had been sent to monitor the annual stocktaking at a timber merchant in Cardiff, South Wales. My job was to check the stock sheets with the physical quantities in the timber yard. As I worked, I had the feeling something was wrong. I found many mistakes; overstatement of quantities, miscalculation of values and wrong casting of stock sheets. What was more unnerving was the fact that the Managing Director seemed to take too much interest in what I was doing, constantly following me about. He was noticeably nervous, and I felt an uncomfortable threat to my safety. I concluded that the stock sheets had been deliberately falsified to inflate the value of the stock. On the second day, I telephoned the partner in charge of the audit. He advised me to return immediately to the office, where he thanked me, and took over the responsibility himself. I later learnt that the Managing Director had been relieved of his post.

In the early summer of 1968, we discovered that Margarita was pregnant. We had been married for ten months. Perhaps the good news would have come earlier, but for a kidney stone that caused a stubborn infection. She had been hospitalised for observation, and surgery had been muted. Fortunately, she was released from hospital without surgery, once it was understood that the condition was hereditary. Both her father and her aunt suffered frequently from kidney stones.

The realisation that she was expecting came one rare evening out. Hugh Stewart was staying with us for the weekend, and we decided to try the dinner dance that was held every Saturday night at the Poultney Hotel. During the meal, Margarita disappeared into the powder room, and was so sick that we had to go home. During the next three months, it was hard for us to go shopping, without her disgracing me in the middle of a crowded street!

Now that we could look forward to our first child, we realised that the lovely flat, in which we had been so happy, was unsuitable for a family, being at the top of several flights of narrow stairs, and no room in the entrance for a pram. So, we started hunting for a house. We became excited by a substantial detached house just outside Bath, with a large garden and an apple orchard. The price was £4,000 but we had saved only about £50. The commitment to a mortgage of such a size frightened us, and we chickened out, going instead for a little box in a terrace in Lower Weston, beside a council estate, close to a disused railway line and just off the A4 to Bristol. Had we had a crystal ball in 1968, we would have seen soaring inflation in the coming years eating into that mortgage debt. Our mortgage repayments would have remained static, we bought the little box for £3,250. We often wondered what might have happened, had we bought the detached house with the orchard!

We moved into No. 17, Westfield Park South in October or November 1968, and prepared for the new addition to the family. Coming from a furnished flat, at first, we had nothing to put in the house. We bought a cooker, a fridge and a mattress, on which we slept on the floor in the bedroom. My parents gave us a utility walnut dining table, chairs and sideboard. We gradually added to the furnishings, with a cheap Conran suite, a beanbag and a brass-plated Victorian bedstead, which we picked up from an antique shop in Bristol, owned by a Spaniard, for an incredible price of £5. It had lain in the shop for a long time. We spent hours cleaning the brass, but we were delighted with the result.

Not having money to spare, I turned to 'do-it-yourself'. I made the kitchen cupboards and sink unit, and the fitted cupboards and bedside tables in the main bedroom, while Margarita, on hands and knees and heavily pregnant, stuck black and white plastic tiles on the kitchen floor. We could not afford proper fitted carpets, but we acquired rolls of heavy-duty beige lining material, which we doubled and fitted in the bedrooms. It was a difficult job, but we had furnished the house having spent very little.

On the 8th January 1969, I went to work in Bristol as usual. Margarita was visiting Ellen, one of our neighbours, when she felt the first contraction. This was around 8 am. Later, she phoned me, and I went home for lunch. Standing at the stove, the pains became stronger, and we knew that the baby was expressing the wish to see daylight. We called the hospital, and they told us to present ourselves. Bath General Hospital was a mere five minutes' drive from the house. Once on our way, the contractions stopped, but we checked in nevertheless. The nursing staff was on some kind of go-slow, and mother and father were left alone. The baby's head appeared at about 3 pm, with very little fuss, and even before the nurses had organised themselves.

Isabel's head was a mass of black hair. We were relieved to see ten fingers and ten toes and an apparently normal baby. I rushed off to the nearest telephone booth, to give the news to the new grandparents; the paternal in Upper Basildon and the maternal in La Coruna. A call to Spain was made through the international operator. I spoke to Don Pio, my father-in-law, in my best Spanish, which was by no means fluent. But thirty seconds was enough to pass the good news of the arrival of his third grand-daughter, and to exhaust my vocabulary! In those days, one had to wait for a look at the genitals to know if the baby was a boy or a girl. Scans were a thing of the future and X-rays were considered harmful to the foetus.

Mother and daughter were home within two days. Life with a new baby in the house was different, but, in common with most couples finding themselves three instead of two, intensely exciting. The camera was never far from the top of the sideboard. Photographs of the firstborn tend to abound, but photography in 1969 was complex and expensive. A celluloid film was loaded, exposed, removed and deposited with the chemist, where it was sent off to be processed. After a week, the prints and the negatives were collected and paid for with hard earned money. Only then would you see the results of your artistic endeavours, if you were lucky. Or you may find the entire film blank and no prints at all! Nowadays, the photo or video is taken by a mobile phone, often to excess, seen one second after clicking, loaded into the computer or deleted if unwanted, and beamed to every part of the world in a few seconds! Such is material progress in a space of fifty-five years. But such progress is often taken for granted.

The first weekend after the baby's discharge from the hospital, we drove to Upper Basildon, to show off the first of a new generation of Hawleys. Just one month after the birth, Nanna Hawley came to Yew Cottage with Auntie

Midge. Photo No. 10 shows Nanna holding baby Isabel. Three other photos of Isabel from March 1969; No. 11 with Nanna Walker, No. 12 with her proud mother, and No. 13 with an unbelieving father.

My mother came to stay with us in Bath for a while. The intention was honourable, but the vibrations in the house were tense. Nineteen-forties English mothers had their ideas, and Spanish nineteen-seventies mothers theirs. Add to the mixture the relationship between mother-in-law and daughter-in-law, and you are bound to have conflict. Mum would have stayed longer, but Margarita managed well and was relieved when she was left alone, to care for her baby the way she instinctively knew how.

In July 1969, my sister, Jean married nineteen-year-old Richard Alexander at the age of twenty, (Photos Nos. 14 & 15). As was the case with my wedding, they were married in Lower Basildon Church and the reception was held at Yew Cottage. Richard's father was a retired army officer, who lived in Upper Basildon with his family and owned an apple orchard.

One visit to my parents' house coincided with the first landing on the Moon. We sat glued to the television set, while Neil Armstrong climbed down the ladder onto the moon's surface and made the historic statement, 'that's one small step for man, one giant leap for Mankind'. It was a historic event, and an incredible feat, since it was only about eight years earlier that the first man had zoomed into space. The achievement was so amazing that there has been plenty of skepticism about NASA's claims to have landed men on the Moon. The photographs sent back from the Moon's surface have been subjected to intense scrutiny. Even today, there are those prepared to say that the film was taken on Earth, and that the Americans staged the most ingenious hoax of the century!

Ever since the 1950's, I had held a special fascination for space exploration. I kept a scrapbook, in which I pasted all newspaper articles featuring space probes, beginning with the first sputnik launched by the Russians in 1958. The scrapbooks came in handy more than forty years later, in providing information for one of my grandchildren's homework project. The bitter cold-war rivalry between the two super powers was undoubtedly the reason for the rapid strides in the exploration of our solar system up to the end of the 1980's. Since the breakup of the Soviet Union, the reduced level of competition has meant a slowdown in the space race.

I drove the car to work in Bristol each day, while Margarita was obliged to wheel the pram to do her shopping. Photo No. 16, taken on the 1st February 1969, shows Margarita with a baby-loaded pram outside the house. It was at least two miles from the centre of Bath, and a tray full of groceries from Sainsbury's beneath the sleeping baby would have been a tiresome load. But to avoid this, on Saturdays, we would often take the car and stock up for the week. Saturday lunch at home invariably consisted of crusty bread, Sainsbury's curd cheese and jam. It was delicious, and always a thing to look forward to. But we tried to vary our diet as much as possible, to the extent that, one day, we decided to make a different dish for dinner every day. And we did that for a good three months! Each meal was recorded in an exercise book, and we made sure no meal was repeated. It was fun, and we experimented with many different recipes. Eating out was expensive for us, and we seldom did, beyond the coffee and hamburger on Poultney Bridge!

In the few years since my childhood, eating habits in Britain had changed considerably. By 1970, fast foods were already in vogue, and restaurant chains such as McDonalds and Burger King were springing up in every town in England. Indian and Chinese restaurants were everywhere. It is said that there are more Indian restaurants in London than in Mumbai! The huge variety and abundance of eastern cooking brought relatively inexpensive and tasty food to those with new-found money in their pockets. Supermarkets were selling TV dinners, pre-cooked packaged meals that only needed heating up; something we didn't often do, fortunately. Gone were the days of overcooked 'meat and two veg'. Of course, there is a negative side. The consumption of processed foods is now considered one of the chief causes of the increased rate of cancer in the modern developed world.

In fine weather, we would sometimes drive out into the beautiful Somerset countryside, and walk to a pub at a convenient distance, making sure we arrived in time for a pint and a packet of crisps, for pubs closed at 2 pm on

Sundays in those days. When Cathy joined us in 1970, Isabel would sit on a seat on top of the reclining Cathy.

The year 1969 provided us with a lovely Indian summer. Cousin Tere brought her family of four small ones; Nico, Ian, Francis and Anthony, to stay with us for a few days, while husband Nicholas attended a naval training course. Even at the beginning of November the days were clear and warm, although the nights were frosty. It was during that visit that Anthony, always the naughty one, locked himself in the bathroom and refused to, or couldn't figure out how to open the door, in spite of all the pleadings. Finally, one of the other boys had to climb in the window of the bathroom.

We became friends with our young, newly-married neighbours. Colin Tavener was a footballer, who played for Trowbridge Town. Ann was a sweet girl. They had a baby boy called Mark, who was roughly the same age as Isabel. He was later joined by his sister, Julie, about the time Isabel acquired her little sister in the spring of 1970. Ann became Isabel's godmother, and gave our daughter her middle name. I will never forget one remark Colin made to us one day. We were talking about condoms. He said with a smile that he hated them, and in his broad West Country accent, he added that it was like ''avin' a barf wiv yer boots on.'

Isabel was duly christened in the church in Upper Basildon, where Mum and Dad sang in the choir. I believe that my brother, John and my sister, Jean were the other godparents. When Cathy came along a year later, we decided to postpone her christening until she was old enough to understand. She finally chose to be baptised at the age of eight.

Since Isabel's birth had been so easy, we decided that Margarita should give birth to number two at home. As was the case with Isabel, we did not know the sex of the infant until the little thing was held up. It was another baby girl. She was born at 3 am on a Sunday morning, the 22nd March 1970. The night before, we were listening to a play on the radio, as we often did on Saturday nights. The play was called 'Gaslight,' a thriller that we later saw on the stage. During the play, contractions started, and the midwife was duly called. The mother-to-be was comfortably installed in a single bed in the back bedroom, and the midwife pulled out her knitting, chatting away while waiting for the action. It was to be a long wait. We telephoned the gynecologist, Dr. Matheson, at the last minute, and he came just in time to see the head of our second daughter emerge from her temporary home. If he had any feelings about being dragged from his bed in the middle of the night he didn't show it. In fact, he was very amenable. Some moments of tension followed, as the baby failed to announce her shock at being thrust into a strange world. She finally cleared her lungs, and we breathed a sigh of relief. Two daughters!

In the morning, Isabel, who was just fourteen-and-a-half months, and who had recently mastered the art of walking, toddled into the room, took one look at her sister and said 'wow-wow.' That was what she thought of her! But I don't remember Isabel ever being unkind to her little sister out of jealousy. But perhaps her initial refusal to be potty-trained was an oblique way of showing her disapproval. We smacked her for that, but it was some time before she obliged. After breakfast on that cold but bright Sunday morning, I burnt the afterbirth on a bonfire in the garden, and we settled down to life with a family of four.

In early April 1970, as soon as Margarita was fully recovered from Cathy's birth, we took her to introduce her to her grandparents. My brother, John also visited Upper Basildon at that time. Photo No. 17 shows him with Margarita in Yew Cottage garden.

The Mini that had given us years of almost trouble-free motoring no longer served a family with two small children. Car seats were highly recommended, if not compulsory by then, and two seats left no room for luggage. So, I bought a Mini Countryman station wagon. The girls became accustomed to being strapped in at an early age, and later, when we travelled long distances, they had already become models of patience.

Isabel as a toddler not only had patience, but concentration far beyond her years. She would sit in front of the dining room sideboard and try to insert the key into the lock of the door. It was painful to watch her, but she hardly ever gave in. Her diligence is evident in Photo No. 18, taken at age 18 months. She was a photogenic child. She had very soon lost the mop of dark hair and had acquired wispy blonde hair instead. Together with her brown eyes and smooth brown skin, she was very pretty; often serious, however. Cathy was also a pretty baby, but she would normally refuse to put on a smile for the camera. In December 1970, before going to work abroad, we hired a professional to take a series of photos of the girls. However many funny faces and noises were directed at her, Cathy's face remained set in a frown. It was not until the frustrated man had finished shooting that the subject gave a smile of satisfaction, (Photo No. 19 of Isabel and No. 20 of Cathy).

I did occasionally have to work away from home. I remember arriving on the doorstep of No. 17 one Friday afternoon, anxious to hold my firstborn, after being away for the whole week. She would not come to me, and cried when I tried to take her from her mother. It was a disappointment. But later, after Cathy was born, Isabel would sometimes reject her mother; out of jealousy perhaps.

Isabel was very sick the first time we fed her fish, and it was not until she was much older that we tried again. Cathy's *bête noir* was eggs, and I must admit we were rather cruel to her, by trying to force her to eat them. I can see her contorted face now, sitting in the highchair. She couldn't bring herself to swallow the egg, but knew she would be very unpopular if she spat it out into her plastic bib!

Three months before Isabel's birth, Margarita and I had bought a fluffy blue toy rabbit in one of the street markets in the East End of London. It had a compartment in which to store pyjamas. That rabbit, and Rabbit was its name, if I am not mistaken, lies on Isabel's bed in reasonable condition after fifty years, and still loved. Later, Cathy also had a rabbit; a pink one called Becky, for which she was mercilessly teased.

In the summer of 1970, we went on holiday for a week to the north coast of Cornwall. Cathy was only three months old, and so was left with her grandparents. The hotel organised entertainment for the evenings, and we met some friendly people. One night, they organised a barbecue on the beach. Isabel was left in the care of a babysitter. Late at night, some of us decided to swim in the sea. The air was cold and the sea even colder. The beach was one of those that sloped very gently, and where the sea retreated far into the distance at low tide. Running down the beach in the pitch black of a moonless night, and wading out through shallow water, Margarita and I wondered whether we would ever reach water deep enough to swim. We two lost sight of the other members of the party. It was a scary experience, and it took us a long time to get warm.

As the year progressed, I became more and more bored with my work, and I considered going into commerce or into business. One venture that interested me at that time was van hire. I reckoned that it was a relatively simple business, and I could see myself doing well at it. However, it needed a large capital investment, and I was not a great risk-taker. I did answer a few advertisements for jobs in the commercial sector without success. In my frustration, I decided to seek work abroad. We had always thought we would be happy in a neutral environment.

The easiest way for me to secure a job abroad was in the profession. Being a Scottish Chartered Accountant I had a head start. The Scottish qualification was considered to be the finest. Large professional firms were always on the look-out for qualified staff with some post-qualifying experience. Throughout the Commonwealth, business and finance had followed the British model, and British trained accountants were in demand. I applied for a position with Cooper Brothers, one of the largest firms of Chartered Accountants in the World. They required qualified audit assistants for their offices in the West Indies. I attended an interview for a post in their Barbados office. Having passed the interview late in 1970, I set about reorganising our lives; handing in my notice at work, selling the car and putting the house in the hands of a letting agent. These arrangements were made by Christmas 1970, and we moved in with my parents at Yew Cottage, safe in the knowledge that we would be sunning ourselves in the Caribbean winter by January 1971. Had we known what was to happen, we would have been in no hurry to sell our car and rent our house!

It was at this time that Britain introduced decimal currency. Mum and Dad had given a home to an elderly lady, who was an old friend of Dorothy and

John Ladd. They would have gladly looked after her, but Dorothy had already taken in her mother. Like all old people faced with a major change, Bee Holland was terrified of decimalisation. She said to us on one of our visits to Yew Cottage that she could not cope with life without her pounds, shillings and pence, and why did they need to change? What was wrong with the old system? Well, it just didn't fit in with the computer age, which was already upon us. Imagine, twelve pennies to a shilling, twenty shillings to one pound and two-hundred-and-forty pennies to the pound! In no time, the people got used to the new currency, and everyone agreed it was easier. Bee passed away not long after this. She no longer had the need for New Pence, had she? As the pace of technological advancement accelerates, old people are having more and more difficulty in coping with life. My mother, for example, would no more have considered having a computer or a mobile phone than fly off to the Moon!

It was in the 1970's that presenting accounts in inflationary times became a serious problem for the Accountancy profession. But after inflation was brought under control, the old historical cost method was once again considered justified. Up to the 1960's, money had kept its value reasonably well. I remember clearly using the big cupronickel penny throughout my childhood, and even into my twenties. Not only that, but pennies were in circulation with six different heads; Elizabeth II, George VI, George V, Edward VII and Queen Victoria. I remember two heads for Queen Victoria; a slim one from what must have been pre-1890's, and the one showing her in old age. By the time of my childhood, those coins had become so worn it was sometimes hard to make out the details.

Attempts were also made in Britain to introduce decimalisation into weights and measures and in the measurement of distances. Kilos are now safely established. In common with the USA, Britain has retained the mile up to today. There was also talk about changing from driving on the left-hand side of the road to driving on the right, a system that is used exclusively on the continent of Europe, and in most other countries in the world. However, perhaps because of the enormous cost of the transition, Britain is still the only country in Europe to drive on the left, Sweden having made the move many years ago.

January passed, and February too, and still we waited for news from Coopers. The problem, said the firm, was in securing a work permit. Apparently, at that time, there was some political wrangling between the UK and some of its Caribbean possessions, or ex-Colonies. Finally, I was offered a job in the St. Lucia office. I accepted that out of desperation. I knew that St. Lucia was a beautiful island but rather small, and I was not sure it would suit us. But it was only to be for two years. As it happened, that did not work out either. By this time, we were becoming frustrated. Life at Yew Cottage was tough for Margarita. With two young children crawling about on doggy-haired carpets, drying nappies in winter weather was no easy task, and Mum objected to nappies being dried on radiators; quite why, I could not understand.

Cooper's gave up the West Indies option and offered me Africa instead; a continent we had not even considered. I was given the choice of Nairobi or Mombasa in Kenya, or Kampala in Uganda. With a brief write-up on the three alternative locations, we deliberated on the different options. In the end, we chose Nairobi, because it was not too far from the sea, and had a more agreeable climate than Mombasa on the coast. We decided Kampala was too far inland. It turned out to be the right choice.

We had stored in a cabin trunk most of the possessions that we had decided to take with us. This had been despatched to a shipping company for storage at the time of moving out of our Bath house, pending our approval for shipment. When I called them to tell them we would be going to Africa instead, they confessed that they had already sent off the trunk to Barbados. So, although we never made it to the West Indies, our trunk did! It was finally returned to the UK, and then shipped off to Kenya, where it arrived in August, more than three months after our arrival in Nairobi.

Having finally settled our future, Margarita, tired of the struggles with my mother, fled with our two children to the comfort of her cousin, Tere's home in Queensferry, on the Firth of Forth near Edinburgh, where her husband had been posted. Cooper's had started paying me, and to give me something to do, sent me on a training course to Birmingham for a week. After that, I decided to join the family in Scotland for Easter.

I chose to hitch hike from Upper Basildon to Queensferry, without a thought for the result of the last unconventional journey I had made to the capital of Scotland. So, very early one cool but sunny day in March, I set off. Dad gave me a lift to the main road to Oxford, and I stuck out my thumb. I got a lift by a motorist to the Oxford Ring Road. From there, a lorry took me to somewhere in the North Midlands by lunchtime, where I remember buying a packet of nuts and raisins. I had to walk with my thumb extended for several miles out of the town and I was feeling a bit dejected. But another lorry stopped and took me all the way to the far North of England, by which time it was dark. I was given a lift in a car for a short distance to a small village, where I went into a pub to raise my spirits. Stepping out into the cold night air, I was lucky to be picked up by a car driver, who was going all the way to Edinburgh. He dropped me in the centre of the City at about midnight, and I called Nicholas, who advised me to get a taxi the ten or so miles to Queensferry, as there was no chance of public transport at that hour. I duly arrived at my destination at 1am, happy and rather proud of my achievement. Hitchhiking in those days was much easier than it is today. With the rise in crime, and fears for their personal safety, drivers are now more inclined to drive past the outstretched thumb.

It was a pleasant stay with the Dolan family. With their four boys and our two girls, there was never a dull moment. One of my strong memories of the stay was the sailing expedition Margarita and I undertook. Nicholas was in charge of the Base's sailing dinghies, and lent one to me one afternoon. The two of us sailed under the Forth Railway Bridge, an exciting moment for me. From there, we could see, to the west the elegant road bridge, which had been opened in 1964. I had not sailed a dinghy since Kuwait days, and it was a chance for me to refresh my memory of the sport.

The Forth Railway Bridge is a major rail link for Eastern Scotland. A contract had been awarded to a prominent civil engineer, Thomas Bouche, who had built the Tay Bridge to the north, but following a tragic accident, in which the Tay Bridge partially collapsed while a train was crossing, the contract was cancelled and given to two English civil engineers; Sir John Fowler and Sir Benjamin Baker. The original suspension bridge idea was scrapped in favour of a cantilever bridge design. Work began on the bridge in 1883, and was opened by the Prince of Wales, later King Edward VII, on the 4th March 1890. It was the first bridge in the world to be built entirely of steel. At two and a half kilometres long, in 1971, it was still the second longest cantilever bridge in the world. The construction was not without tragedy. A staggering ninety-eight workers lost their lives, and four-hundred-and-fifty were injured. Even today, the Forth Bridge is considered a great feat of engineering, and is a UNESCO world heritage site. The bridge needs constant maintenance and a permanent depot, with housing for the more than fifty workmen stands on the northern shore. There exists a popular myth, claiming that the bridge is constantly being painted. By the time the workmen reach one end, it is time to start painting the other end! It is untrue. The very first painting contract was not awarded until 2002. The work involved the removal of all the existing paint and the application of twenty-thousand square metres of paint. The work was to be completed in ten years at a cost of one-hundred-and-eighty-million pounds. But at least the job will not need doing for an estimated forty years! I wonder what the entire bridge cost in 1890!

Back in Berkshire, we prepared to start a new life in the tropics. Work permit secured, we booked our flights for the 5th May with East African Airways. Our intention at that time was to stay in Nairobi for two years and, with overseas experience under my belt, to come back to the UK, to pursue my career in the Profession, or in Commerce and Industry. Little did we know that Africa can be very alluring, and too long in its sway can grip the unwary, so that tearing oneself away can be very difficult indeed. Little did we know that Kenya was eventually to become our permanent home!

John had recently met his future wife, Cathy, a New Zealander. At the time of our departure, they were working in London. Their wedding took place in the summer of 1972. I flew from Kenya for the wedding unannounced. Three photos are displayed; No. 21, showing the bride and groom, No. 22 with Mum and Dad and I, and No. 23 with Nanna and Grandad Walker. After their marriage in 1972, they were to move permanently to Auckland, leaving my parents with only their daughter near them. My mother must have felt the pain of these events, having spent so many years in Kuwait, while looking forward to having her three children close to her one day. But children have their lives to lead, and parents have to accept this. I believe my mother did accept it, but perhaps she would have wanted it a different way.

No. 1

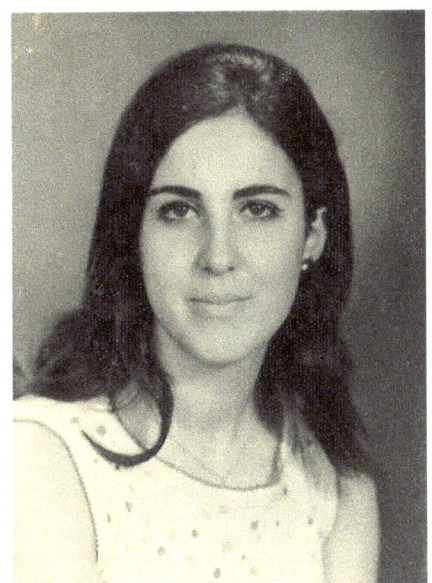
No. 2

Mr. & Mrs. Charles Hawley
request the pleasure of

Company at the marriage of their son
Christopher to Margarita García López
at St. Bartholomew's Church, Lower Basildon, Berks,
on Saturday, 9th September at 2 p.m.
and afterwards at Yew Cottage, Upper Basildon.

Yew Cottage,
 Upper Basildon,
  Reading, Berks.

No. 3

No. 4

No. 5

No. 6

No. 7

No. 8

No. 9

No. 10

No. 11

No. 12

No. 13

No. 14

No. 15

No. 16

No. 17

No. 18

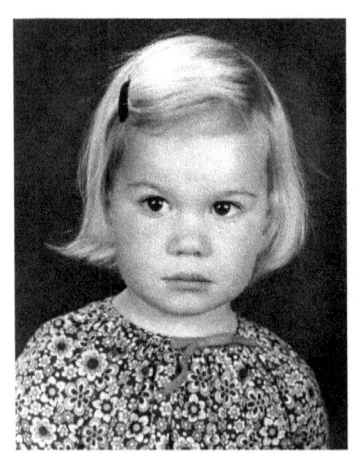
No. 19

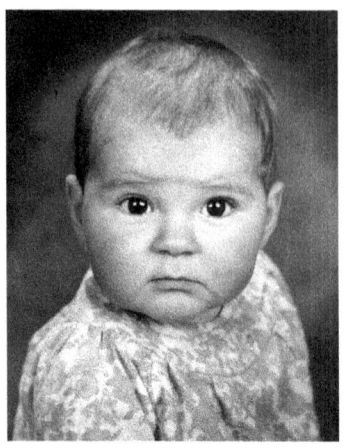
No. 20

No. 21

No. 22

No. 23

AFRICAN EXPERIENCE

Nairobi

THE EAST AFRICAN AIRWAYS VC10 landed at Entebbe Airport on its way to Nairobi, carrying, among others, a pair of excited adventurers and two bewildered little girls. And it was there that our suitcase was accidentally offloaded. Landing in Nairobi with two little ones dressed in clothes smelling of vomit, and without a change of clothes, was not a good start. However, we were met at Embakasi Airport by an employee of the firm for which I had eagerly agreed to work, and taken to Brunner's, an old-fashioned hotel in the centre of the City, where we spent our first day and night on Kenyan soil; the 6th May 1971.

I often wonder what course our lives would have taken, had we opted for a job in Mombasa or Kampala, rather than choosing Nairobi. We had rejected Mombasa as being too hot, and Kampala as being too far from the sea. It turned out to be a fortuitous choice. Nairobi is a culturally diverse city, with plenty of opportunities for a full life. Mombasa is on the sea, but is far smaller, and with limited possibilities for non-work-related activities, apart from beach and sea-related pastimes. Kampala is a pleasant city, but there was another factor, which we could not have known in 1971. Idi Amin was shortly to stage a coup against President Milton Obote, and begin a despotic rule. In 1972, he deported all Asians with British passports, crippling an economy largely run by Asian businessmen. But who knows; perhaps we would have been given a transfer to Nairobi.

Brunner's Hotel was a typical example of the colonial atmosphere that still prevailed in Nairobi seven-and-a-half years after Independence. Brunner's was demolished many years ago now. The double doors of our first-floor room opened onto a simple walled verandah that overlooked Kaunda Street, at the junction with Muindi Mbingu Street. But Nairobi has changed since then. The state of security in Nairobi nowadays would not allow for an open verandah, unprotected by bars, and or toughened glass windows. Rooms were sprayed with a spray gun before dusk to keep mosquitoes away. On the ground floor, a simple, cosy restaurant and a spacious lounge bar, furnished with mock upholstered leather reclining chairs, opened liberally onto Kaunda Street.

Nairobi was founded in 1899. At that time, it was a depot for the railway that was being constructed by the British East Africa Company, from the port of Mombasa to Port Florence, (now Kisumu), on Lake Victoria. The railway was a clear vision on the part of the architects, but many contemporaries could not fathom why anyone would want to construct a railway line through uninhabited bush, halfway across Africa to nowhere in particular. This gave rise to the name, 'Lunatic Express'.

Nairobi, which in the Masai language means 'place of cool water', was situated at the boundary between the plains, home to the pastoral Maasai, and the forested slopes, the domain of the Kikuyu, the most numerous of Kenya's tribes. True to its name, it was nothing but a swamp, inhabited by very few people, but many wild animals, and trillions of mosquitoes. But Nairobi quickly grew, and by 1904 boasted a railway station, the famous Norfolk Hotel, a bazaar, and some permanent houses on the hill. Those staying in the Norfolk Hotel might wake up in the night to the sound of marauding lions, or sit and sip their beers on the verandah, while watching game drinking at the waterhole right in front of them. Up to that time, Machakos, some sixty or so kilometres towards Mombasa, had been the capital of the British Colony, but Nairobi became the capital in 1905. By the time of our arrival in 1971, Nairobi had grown into a city of more than three-quarters-of-a-million people, but still retained its provincial atmosphere. Well over eighty per cent of Kenya's fifteen million people lived a rural life, and the mass influx of job-seekers from the rural areas, believing that the streets of Nairobi were lined with gold, had hardly begun. Nairobi City centre was free of the crowds that today throng the streets, and parking was unrestricted. Few Africans owned cars at that time. The main streets of the business district were lined with flowering shrubs and trees, and the pavements still held together. Destitute citizens and orphaned children had not taken to roaming the streets as they do today, and walking around the City centre after dark was still a relatively safe pastime. How Nairobi has deteriorated in the fifty-odd years since then!

In 1971, the Kenyatta International Conference Centre was being completed, and dominated the skyline. There were no other buildings anywhere near approaching its height. Suburban shopping and business centres had not begun to sprout, and supermarkets were only in their infancy. The European community lived mainly in leafy suburbs to the north and west of the City. The bulk of the growing African population lived to the east and south, many in makeshift housing developments. The other main racial group, the Asians; Indians and Pakistanis, but mainly Guajarati, lived chiefly in the inner suburbs of Parklands and Westlands. We had been allocated a maisonette in Westlands, about three kilometres from the city centre.

Cooper Brothers had given me a small loan to buy my first car, since we were advised that it was essential to be independent of public transport. All expatriates owned a car. On my first morning in Nairobi, I walked down Parliament Road, past the National Assembly buildings, to Cooper Motors, where I was told that I could find a reasonably priced, reliable secondhand car. I chose a VW Variant station wagon for Shs.4,500/-. I believe that was the price. I drove for some time on my UK driving licence, before being given the archaic red cardboard Kenya licence, that was still in use more than forty years on, and that fell to pieces in no time at all!

Having become mobile, we were taken to our new home in Mpaka Grove, at the end of Third Avenue Parklands. We were to occupy the upper floor of a two-story house that had been converted into two dwellings. It had a substantial garden, mainly covered with grass, with a few trees and some flower beds near the house. We had arrived in the middle of the long rains, and I remember the extensive pools, through which little Cathy would love to run, in the company of the small son of the house servant. Our downstairs neighbours, Andrew and Jane Little, became longtime friends, despite the suspicion that they had selected the best furniture from the two maisonettes and left us with the rubbish! But perhaps we would have done the same in their situation. We were unhappy with the condition of the house and furniture, especially the rusty bathtub and the blue plastic three-piece suite with ugly wooden arms. We said as much to Malcolm Pedlow, the partner in charge, but only some things were attended to. However, we enjoyed the large garden and the roof space, especially the girls. In Photo No. 24, a smiling Isabel rides her tricycle on the open verandah, and in Photo No. 25, Isabel and Cathy enjoy the fresh Nairobi air. Photo No. 26 was taken in the Mpaka Grove garden in December 1972, just before we moved house.

Andrew and Jane soon found themselves a house in Lenana Road, and a new couple moved into the maisonette below us, without any suspicion that the best furniture had been removed! David McDonald had also come to Kenya on contract with Cooper's, with his very young New Zealand wife, Carrie. They also became good friends. Later, on leaving the firm, he started KATE, a freight and forwarding business that still exists today.

Cooper Brothers & Co. had their offices in Queensway House, at the far end of Kaunda Street from Brunner's Hotel, and I believe they still occupy the same premises. The partners, senior managers and qualified staff were all White, mainly expatriate British men, except for one or two Indian qualified assistants. The trainee audit clerks were mainly African. You would be hard put to find an expatriate among the staff of Coopers & Lybrand today! The professional class of Kenyans has grown to such an extent in the past fifty years that work permits are given only to highly qualified foreigners with special skills, subject to some corruption here and there. When I worked with Cooper's, it was the expatriates of the firm and their wives that formed the social circle, in which we spent much of our leisure hours.

Having moved into our maisonette, it was time to start work. My first audit was at Jubilee Insurance Company in Jubilee House, Wabera Street, just a short walk from the office. Having not worked for almost five months, it was very hard to apply my mind to dealing with figures during those first few days. After some panicky hours, in which I struggled to churn a rusty brain into action, I began to settle down to the work. During my eighteen months with the Firm, I enjoyed working on a variety of audits, dealing with companies in tea and ranching, light manufacturing, timber and dealerships, among others. The group that owned tea estates and ranches offered me the chance to see some interesting places while on the job.

One of the first decisions to be made was; which social and sports club should we join? Clubs tended towards exclusivity, The Goan Gymkhana for the Goans, The Sikh Union for the Sikhs and so on. Later, clubs were forced to change their names in the interests of racial harmony, so that The Goan Gymkhana became The Gymkhana Club and The Sikh Union became The Simba Union. It was a cosmetic measure that did little to change the membership of the clubs. Three clubs in which most expatriate Europeans felt at home were Parklands Sports Club, Nairobi Club and Muthaiga Club. Parklands Club was the one to which most of my work colleagues belonged, and so we joined, at a fee of Shs.700/-, I believe. It had a good swimming pool, tennis and squash courts, a rugby-cum-cricket field, a hockey pitch, a billiard room, and a bar and restaurant. In faded Photo No. 27, Isabel and Cathy sunbathe by the pool. In those days, the membership was practically all White, with a few Asians. Slowly, as the number of expatriate Europeans reduced, so the mix included more Asians. Later, the membership of the club became predominantly Asian. Nowadays, it is the well-to-do Africans, and chiefly Kikuyu, that make up well over 90% of the membership. But it is the latter group that has transformed the club into a top-class social and sports club. A member who left Kenya in 1971 would hardly recognise it now as the place where he spent his Sundays with the family, or where he enjoyed a beer after work during the week. The fee for joining the club now is, I believe, something in the region of Shs.250,0000/-.

Nairobi Club and Muthaiga Club remained White-dominated clubs for many years, but there are few expatriates left in Kenya now. The pool at

Impala Club was always badly kept. I think we were invited only once by a friend. It was like swimming in soup! Nowadays, if the White Kenyans belong to a club, it would probably be Karen Club, which prides itself on an excellent golf course. But the Karengata community, (Karen and Lang'ata), keep themselves to themselves, by and large. We, as an expatriate community, hardly ever came across them. The 'Kenya Cowboys', as they are impolitely called, are comfortable in their niche. They are involved chiefly in farming, tourism, horticulture and cottage industries.

Apart from weekends spent at the club, there was always the Safari. At least once a month, we would pack up the car with a tent, sleeping bags and cooking equipment, and head off into the bush. We very soon found the Variant to be unsuitable for such expeditions with two small children, and we swapped it for a VW Kombi Camper van, KKK 197, fitted out with eating and sleeping facilities, (see Photo No. 28, in which the van is being refuelled on one safari to Lake Baringo). In those days, there were so many wild and exciting places to visit; not only National Parks, but sparsely populated bush country, where the local people accepted our presence, occasionally coming to stand and stare, before returning to the occupation in which they had been involved. We never felt a threat, from people or animals. We camped in almost all the National Parks and Reserves, as well as on the shores of Lake Magadi, Lake Chala and Lake Turkana. We camped in the Chyulu Hills, the Aberdare Mountains, the Nguruman Escarpment, the Maralal Forest, and even in a carpark in the heart of Kisumu Town! Camping today is unsafe, unless in designated camping sites. This is particularly true anywhere near populated areas. I will later select a few camping experiences that will give an idea of the thrills of our first five years in Kenya.

We had been in Kenya for eight months when my mother paid her first visit. Dad stayed behind in England. It was January and we were enjoying hot weather. One trip I remember taking with Mum was up north to Samburu. We have a movie film, in which she is holding a cup of tea, and gazing across at Mt. Kenya, its snowcapped top clearly visible in the cool morning air. We often visited Samburu in the years that followed. It is on the edge of what used to be called the Northern Frontier District before we arrived in Kenya. At that time, one had to obtain permission to enter the NFD, because it was the home of bandits, or *shifta,* as they are called in Kiswahili. Samburu National Park held several species of animal not found further south: the Grevy's Zebra, the Gerenuk and the Reticulated Giraffe being the best known.

We visited other nearer places of interest with my mother, such as Lake Naivasha. She was a keen bird watcher, and was happy to sit for hours with a pair of binoculars. Over five hundred species of bird have been recorded around Lake Naivasha. In the years that followed, my interest in ornithology became a passion. Over the years, I have studied the birdlife in many locations in Kenya.

I took some leave days for an excursion into Tanzania, our first into that country. In Photo No. 29, Margarita and I are sitting inside the van. We drove down to Namanga on the border, slept the night there in the car park of the hotel, and then drove the long, straight and narrow road southwards towards Arusha. Off to the left, the snow-covered summit of Mt. Kilimanjaro was just visible through the clouds. The free-standing Mt. Meru appeared in the distance ahead of us, and as we approached it, the van seemed to labour. I felt sure the engine was losing power, until I understood that we were in fact climbing a long steep hill. The presence of the mountain in front of us gave the impression that we were cruising along on level ground. However, by the time we had reached the turning west towards Lake Manyara, the engine was overheating, and we stopped in a petrol station to allow it to cool. We finally entered Lake Manyara National Park in time for a swim in the pool of the lodge, situated precariously on top of a hill overlooking the lake.

The National Park is home to a wide variety of animals. Lions there have picked up the habit of climbing trees, something they do not generally do. Our most exciting experience took place in the evening, parked in the campsite. We were preparing to retire to bed. I was brushing my teeth in the shadows, not far from the van, when there in a nearby clearing, in stark moonlight, a rhinoceros was grazing peacefully, completely unaware of my presence. We watched the huge animal from the roof hatch of the camper for some time. It had no idea we were there.

The audit of the group of companies that owned tea estates and a cattle ranch gave me the opportunity to see some wild and wonderful places. I was sent to Kericho for a couple of weeks, to check the records and review the systems at the Kaisugu tea factory. I stayed in the director's house, and was treated like one of the family. I remember those clear, sunny, crisp Highland mornings that give way to cloudy afternoons, with heavy showers and frequent thunder storms. In those conditions, tea grows well. I watched the fascinating process of 'tea making', in which the leaves are shredded, fermented and finally dried. The final product is graded and tasted, to ensure it meets the required standard.

The audit of the cattle ranch was an even greater adventure. The ranch was situated way out on the Laikipia plateau, a long way north of Rumuruti. I was given permission to take the family along with me. With directions to the ranch, we set off in the Kombi van, passing through Naivasha, Nakuru and Thomson's Falls, (now Nyahururu). After leaving that small market town, with its impressive waterfall bearing the name of the Scottish explorer, Joseph Thomson, the dirt road cuts through a forested area, before descending to the open plain of Laikipia. We reached this point as night was closing in, but we continued on the small track, which we believed would take us to our destination. We were tired. As we chugged on into the night, straining to pick up obstacles in the headlights, we became increasingly concerned that we may not be on the right road after all. The journey seemed endless, but finally, after we had almost given up hope, we saw the lights of a ranch house ahead. We were very relieved to be there.

Colin Francombe and his red-headed wife gave us a warm welcome and a meal, for which we were grateful. They were very hospitable, and treated us like family for the whole time we were there. We elected to sleep in the van, although I have no doubt we could have stayed in the house if we had wished. It was difficult to concentrate on the work I was obliged to do; working in a little round building among the outhouses. It was hot during the day, and the sounds and sights of the busy homestead were a distraction to someone needing to keep his attention on words and figures.

Isabel and Cathy had a good time. There were several pet animals that wandered freely about the farmyard, notably a young buffalo and a baby bush pig, as well as dogs, ducks and chickens. The buffalo was inclined to be playful, and the girls were wary of it. After work one day, we piled into the back of Colin's Land Rover and drove out into the bush, Colin and his wife armed with shotguns. Yellow-necked spurfowl was the common game bird in the area. On our way, we met some of the native people who lived on the ranch. The Pokot is a small tribe of dark-skinned pastoralists. They are known for their warlike nature. The women were heavily decorated with necklaces and bangles. I had a movie camera and took some film of them. I did meet Colin in Lamu some years ago. He was not the tall and skinny youth whom I remembered from 1972. He had filled out and lost hair. Why is it that when we meet people we've not seen for many years, we always expect them to look the same, and are surprised if they have aged?

Colin Francombe featured in Kuki Gallman's book, 'I dreamed of Africa'. He became the manager of the ranch that she bought in Laikipia with her husband, Paulo. The book tells the true and tragic tale of her struggle with life, with a husband who had a passion for hunting and a son who was fascinated by snakes. Paolo was killed by an elephant, while Emmanuelle was bitten by one of his pet snakes and died in his mother's arms. She was left with a daughter, and later lived in Nairobi. But she dedicated her life to conservation of the wildlife and the environment of Laikipia.

Anne and Philip Dobson were the closest friends we had in our first five years in Kenya, and it was with them that we mostly went on Safari. Philip worked for the same firm as I did. After a two-year contract, in common with most of us, he left the profession for the greener pastures of commerce. When I did the same in January 1973, we remained close friends and camping colleagues. Anne was a trained nurse and a no-nonsense one; matron material for sure! When they left Kenya around 1980, they presented us with a photo album, containing one or more snaps taken during each of the safaris we had done together. In Photo No. 30, Anne and Phil sit with their two children, Caroline and Mark.

One of the most memorable weekends with them was spent on the Nguruman escarpment in March 1974, (Photo No. 31). It was a long journey, around the Ngong Hills, down into the spectacular Rift Valley, past Olorgasale, the site of important fossil remains, and down to the furnace that is Lake Magadi, in a depression less than two-thousand feet above sea level. The Lake can be seen from far, its white soda ash brilliant white in the sunlight. The entire lake is covered metres thick with the salt crust, extracted and refined by the Magadi Soda Company. It is one of the hottest places in Kenya. When Nairobi is deep in the cloud and chill of winter, Magadi is the place to go to feel the sun's heat. Leaving the lake, we followed the stony track, through thorn bush towards the west, then south along the river, until Lake Natron appeared in the distance, across the border in Tanzania. The track took a right turn, and up the escarpment into another world. Nguruman, backed by the Loita Hills, is like the Garden of Eden; lush green, with high grass and fever trees, and swarming with animals. Hardly a soul ventured there in those days: it was way off the tourist routes. We saw herds of buffalo, lions in the trees, and the sound of hyenas kept us company at night. It was also home to the tsetse fly; those annoying beasts that sting through your socks when you are driving. They were also the reason why it is not an area favoured by cattle owners, since tsetse flies carried sleeping sickness.

Philip Leakey, a son of the famous paleontologists, Louis and Mary Leakey, and brother to the well-known Richard Leakey, had built an impressive tree house near where we were camping. Incidentally, Richard was the one who had discovered human fossils more than two-million years old. His father had declared that the area around Lake Turkana was the 'Cradle of Mankind', and Mary had discovered important fossil remains in the Olduvai Gorge in Tanzania. Richard went on to head the Kenya Wildlife Service, and at one time held the Government position of Secretary to the Cabinet, until he put his nose too deeply into corruption scandals, and almost paid for it with his life.

The Collins was another family with whom we became very good friends during our stay in Mpaka Grove. Arthur and Jennifer lived around the corner in Livingstone Drive, (now General Mathenge Drive). They had three daughters somewhat older than ours. Arthur enjoyed nothing better than pulling an engine to bits. He took out the VW engine when I had a problem. We camped once with them in Amboseli during very hot, dry weather. I have a film of Arthur, driving his Datsun SSS through the dust, and sending up clouds of the fine, white powder. A few years later, they became close friends with another couple, going in for the perilous practice of wife-swapping. Arthur ended up going off with Margaret and leaving his wife and children. I believe Margaret, although not beautiful, must have given him the satisfaction that perhaps Jennifer was unable to give him. Jennifer and Margaret's husband were not so much attracted to each other, and never became a couple. The last we heard of Jennifer was that she was living alone in the UK. Margaret's husband eventually died of throat cancer. We never heard what happened to Arthur and Margaret, and I often wonder whether he regretted losing his family for the sake of an 'exciting' woman!

One Christmas, we joined several couples for a camping expedition to the Chyulu Hills. This range of green hills, waterless and therefore inhabitant-less, stretch almost from Amboseli National Reserve to Tsavo National Park, the track from one to the other passing alongside the hills. Driving from Kibwezi to Mtito Andei towards Mombasa, they can be seen over to the right. From the top, one has one of the finest views of Mt. Kilimanjaro. In a hollow, on the side of the hills facing Africa's highest mountain, we camped for four nights. In Photo No. 32, Margarita and I, with Andrew Little and Phil Dobson, admire the wonderful view. During this time, we saw not a single soul. We attempted to roast a whole piglet on a spit over the campfire. This was our Christmas lunch, but it became our supper instead. The pig refused to cook and, in the end, we had to cut it up and roast it that way. What with the heat from the fire and the rays from a blazing December sun, I cooked more than the pig! (see Photo No. 33).

In 1973, my father took the first of several holidays in Kenya, always with

Mum to accompany him. Their visits usually coincided with the English winter, Kenya's summer. Although Kenya straddles the equator, it is surprising how different July is from, say January or February. Every year, Nairobi residents complain of the cold in July, and then the heat in February and March, declaring that they have never known it so cold, or so hot.

One very exciting trip was made to Masai Mara. We still had the Kombi, so it must have been the first time Mum and Dad came to Kenya together. We camped in the official campsite just outside the park gate, on the way in from Narok. Margarita and I slept in the little orange tent, which had served us faithfully for years, while my parents slept in the VW with the children. During the night, a large pride of lions killed a giraffe, a fact we did not come to know until the morning. The male lion, who always eats his fill first, roared loudly to keep away the females and other scavengers from the kill. Lying with our ears to the ground, the lions could have been just outside our thin tent. We spent an uncomfortable night, expecting a set of claws to rip the fragile fabric at any moment. The next morning, we located the kill, and were surprised at how far from our tent it was; at least four-hundred yards away, and the lions were far too interested in eating giraffe than eating skinny humans!

What did our little girls think of the camping expeditions? They were certainly no trouble, although they were forced to spend hours in the back of the VW Camper van. They were sometimes so quiet that we hardly knew they were there. There was one time we were passing Thika, where the pineapples grow, in the camper, and we decided to stop for some. For just one shilling you could pick up two or three pineapples. Driving away from the sellers, on our way back to Nairobi, Margarita, from the passenger seat, suddenly alerted me that Isabel, who was about five years old, was not in the back. I immediately turned the car and raced back towards the place where we had bought the pineapples, thinking we had left her there on the side of the road. I think Cathy, one year younger than her sister, must then have said something. We stopped the car, and opened the cover of one of the bench seats, to find Isabel hiding there. We laughed, with relief.

Writing about Thika reminds me of the time we took Mum and Dad to see the spectacular Fourteen Falls, near Thika. A thief attempted, unsuccessfully, to snatch Mum's handbag, and she landed in the bushes. There was no damage but she had a fright. Thika must have been jinxed for us. Another Sunday, we took a trip to the same falls with the Dobson family. They had a VW camper van similar to ours. Their presence turned out to be a blessing. I was taking an innocent movie film downstream, while two men were crossing the river in a small rubber boat. We were preparing to get into our vehicles, when the two men appeared, and announced that they were plain-clothes policemen, and that it was an offence to take pictures of policemen. We argued that we had not even known they were policemen, since they had no uniforms, and I was merely taking a film of the river. As we were talking we were shoving the girls into the car, hoping to make a getaway, but one of the men produced a gun and told me I was under arrest. At that point, Phil said he would report the matter to the Thika Police Station. While he and Anne were away, we were not allowed to move. Finally, after about an hour, they returned, having reported it to the officer in charge. To cut a long story short, we were escorted to the police station, where the boss dismissed the case as a piece of nonsense, and let us go. It was a nervous time.

In January 1973, I left Cooper's. After eighteen months with the firm, it was clear that there were more interesting and better-paid positions in commerce. The business community was small, and expatriates from the different sectors mixed freely. It was not difficult therefore to secure a job. I was interviewed by Ken Warrilow, the Managing Director for Westlands Motors, a company in the Lonrho Group holding the dealership for Toyota motor vehicles, for the post of Chief Accountant. The salary was more attractive than that paid by Cooper's, and the added perk of a free car as well as free weekend transport was too good to refuse. Most of my expatriate colleagues were making similar moves. Cooper's demanded compensation for breaking a two-year contract, which Ken Warrilow gladly paid.

Our newly rented house in Davidson Road, now Rhapta Road, was an improvement on the maisonette that Cooper's had provided. It was a low bungalow, with three bedrooms and an office, a large kitchen and a long sitting/dining room, with a fireplace at one end. A covered verandah in front gave onto a pretty garden. We lived there and loved there until we returned to the UK in 1976. A delightful Photo No. 34, of Isabel and Cathy in the verandah, was taken in December 1973. The Company provided a car for my use; a yellow Toyota 2000. Later, I was given a Toyota Celica, in which we once clocked 160 kms per hour on the Mombasa Road; never to be repeated!

The work was more interesting too. I reported directly to the Managing Director, and supervised an accounts department of about eight staff. Toyota was a top selling make of car, and the Company did well. At one time, a new Corolla cost under Shs.30,000, the shilling being worth a lot more then than it is today. The shilling was on a par with the old British shilling; twenty to the pound, but at one time it appreciated to thirteen shillings to the pound, and at that time the Company made a killing! The poor old battered dollar was only worth seven shillings!

The managing Director of the Lonrho Group in Kenya was Udi Gecaga, pronounced 'Gechaga', the grandson of Jomo Kenyatta, Kenya's first President. Udi's father, B. M. Gecaga had married a daughter of *Mzee* Kenyatta. Udi was a likeable young man, but to me not a strong personality, and I wonder how much his appointment was a political expedient, to oil the wheels of Tiny Roland's African business empire. My immediate boss on the financial level was Jeff Austen-Brown, whom I can thank for giving me the job at Westlands Motors. Jeff was a supportive superior and we met many times socially.

My brother, John, and his wife, Cathy came to visit us in December 1974; their first and last. Did they find the 1974/75 safaris too adventurous to risk another visit? We certainly took them on some hairy scary trips! Like the weekend we spent around Maralal. Having visited the frontier town, in the heart of Samburu country, and lunched at the Maralal Lodge, we drove out towards North Horr, up to the top of the escarpment, from where the sandy road winds down into the Rift Valley, and then on to Lake Turkana. As the sun was setting, we turned back and found a side track, which entered a forested area. It was quiet, and we decided to camp there. From the trees hung long trails of grey-green lichen, which took on a sinister aspect in the light of the campfire, as soon as darkness descended. After eating and safely tucked up in our sleeping bags, John and Cathy in one tent and we four in the other, we looked forward to a silent night. Then the barking started. What were the animals that yelped all around us? Were they wild dogs, jackals or something more terrible? Come morning, and in the comfort of daylight, we felt better. Only later did we come to learn that the animals that yelped were only zebra! If we had been nervous, you can imagine how John and Cathy felt!

Other expeditions with John and Cathy were to Samburu Reserve, Mt. Kenya, Meru National Park and to Lamu. The Samburu trip was memorable for the song Cathy made up, which went like this: 'We are going on safari and it's very very *kali,* singing polly-wolly-doodle all the day......' This was sung to the tune of Polly-Wolly-Doodle. In Kiswahili, *kali* means violent, or strong, or sharp or spicy. On Mt. Kenya, we parked the car at the Meteorological Station at ten-thousand feet, and walked up into the forest. Cathy took Photo No. 35 of my family with John. In Meru National Park we stayed in *bandas,* which are small cottages. Meru was one of the parks where endangered white rhinos were being relocated from other areas. They had become so tame one could actually stroke them. To prove this statement, Photo No. 36, taken during a later visit to Meru National Park, shows our girls stroking a baby rhino.

The trip that I enjoyed the most was the exciting one we took to Lamu. A long wheelbase Land Cruiser Station Wagon allowed the six of us to travel in comfort, with all the camping gear we needed. We drove down the Mombasa road to Voi, two thirds of the way to the coast, and entered Tsavo East National Park, where we camped the first night. One of the joys of camping in Africa is the freedom to enjoy a campfire, with as much dry *kuni* (firewood) as you could ever need. The weather was hot, but at least the evenings were cooler. The next morning, we continued through the park. Tsavo East is enormous, and is home to many elephants. Beyond the park, the road descends to Malindi, through the deepest dust I have ever seen. From there, where Vasco Da Gama had landed in 1498, the dirt road runs northwards to the little town of Garsen, where Somalis, Pokomos and other northern tribes mingle. A causeway has since been built to allow traffic to reach Lamu, when the Tana River spreads its waters over the delta, but in 1975, vehicles crossed the river by means of a tiny ferry, which was operated manually by means of rope pulleys. That delightful experience over, we continued north-eastward to Mokowe, by way of Witu. The entire journey from Malindi was about two-hundred-and-forty kilometres and took the best part of the day. At the present time, the road is tarred and the ferry is a forgotten dream.

We left the vehicle in the care of a car park attendant at Mokowe and boarded a motor dhow to Lamu town, a journey of about forty minutes. We arrived exhausted, and were glad to find a little hotel in the centre of the town; Mahrus Hotel. In those days, Lamu was not the well-known tourist destination it is today; more the haunt of the hippies. There were few hotels in the town, but many cheap guest houses, where one could sleep for very little. With cheap eating houses, low-budget travellers could stay for weeks. Mahrus Hotel rooms were small, but we only paid ninety shillings, (about five sterling pounds at that time). Our room overlooked the local prison, which occupied one wing of the Lamu Fort. The prison was later moved to Hindi on the mainland. The Fort is now used for cultural functions and houses offices.

The Lamu Archipelago is a group of islands off the Kenyan coast, about a hundred kilometres south-west of the border with Somalia. It comprises three main islands; Lamu, Manda, Pate, as well as several smaller ones, notably Kiwayu. Much of the shoreline is covered by mangrove swamps, but facing the ocean there are sandy beaches.

We stayed for three or four days. On at least one of the days, John and Cathy, Margarita and I and the two girls walked along the beach to Shela, a little Swahili village about three kilometres from the town, and on the point facing Ras Kitau, the southern end of Manda Island. Years later, this quaint village was to become our second home, although at that time we could have had no idea of this.

I do not remember much of our visit to Shela on that day, when 1974 had given way, or was about to give way, to 1975. But I do remember that the tide was low, revealing an expanse of green seaweed. We must have refreshed ourselves at the Peponi Hotel bar, and we must have swum in the warm sea, before returning to Lamu town. We did not think of venturing into the little village behind Peponi Hotel. At that time, Shela was no more than a collection of simple one-story houses, and ruins of more substantial structures from the time when Shela was home to a prosperous community.

Peponi Hotel was, at that time, the only hotel in Shela, occupying a prominent position on the headland, at the beginning of the twelve-kilometre-long beach. The hotel had been founded in 1967 by a Danish couple. Later, the son, Lars Korschen, took over the management of the hotel with his wife, Carol. On the death of Lars, Carol continued to run the hotel until 2023, when her two daughters entered the scene. Substantial improvements have recently been made. Peponi is internationally known and was, at that time, listed among the Hundred Best Hotels of the World. Today, there are many hotels, private houses and guest houses in the village. In the 1980's, we spent several holidays in Shela, and once on Manda Island in a house on sparsely populated Ras Kitao belonging to Paddy and Denys Allen, (Photo No. 37). They were away at the time, and allowed us to use the house. We particularly liked Coconut House in Shela, close to the beach, and it was while staying there in 1989 that we met Abdullahi Shekuwe, and decided to buy our own plot. I was to run a hotel in conjunction with Abdullahi in the 1990's.

Our thirst for adventure was apparently insatiable during those first five years in Kenya. Perhaps our most intrepid venture into the wilderness was the time we borrowed the Company long wheelbase Land Cruiser, the same one which had taken us to Lamu, and drove to Lake Turkana and back across the Chalbi Desert to Marsabit. Unfortunately, no photos of the memorable journey are available.

I had been advised to treat the insides of the tyres with a solution to protect them from punctures. It was a wise move. We did not have a single puncture during the entire journey, and we traversed some very rough terrain. Dropping down the escarpment into the Rift Valley, north of Maralal, we began to experience the searing heat of the semi-desert. A hot and tiring journey faced us that second day. The girls, still small, were used to travelling long distances, and I don't remember them complaining much. I would not have blamed them if they had done. It must have been boring for them to spend so many hours in the back of the Land Cruiser. Finally, we reached the volcanic lava flows, which brought us to the crest of a hill, from where the Jade Sea was stretched out before us.

Lake Turkana is one-hundred kilometres long and Kenya's largest lake, (excluding Lake Victoria, which is shared with Uganda, Rwanda, Burundi and Tanzania). Turkana is a fresh water lake and abounds in fish. Its northern end abuts the Ethiopian border, where the Omo River flows into the lake. The area around the lake was the scene of intense archeological excavation, and Professor Louis Leakey declared that it was possibly the 'Cradle of Mankind.' Into this wilderness we drove that day. We were tired and thirsty. Fortunately, there is a lodge at Loengalani, not far from the lake shore, and I can imagine we stopped at the bar, before continuing to the shore to find a camping place.

The first night there was extremely uncomfortable. A strong, hot and dry wind blew off the lake all evening, making it very difficult to keep sand out of the food we were trying to cook on the campfire. In the end, we retired to bed without supper and nursing headaches; at least, I was suffering from a severe one. So, the next day, we sought out the manager of Loengalani Lodge, and pleaded with him to allow us to camp inside the grounds of the lodge. He was a pleasant Samburu and he agreed. We entered through a gateway at the rear of the lodge and erected our tent. There we were comfortable, sheltered from the wind. We revelled in the cool water of the little swimming pool, and the cool beer from the bar as well no doubt!

The next day or the day after, the holiday almost ended in disaster. We were returning from a local trip about lunchtime. We passed through the gate and were crossing the compound, when, all of a sudden, the ground gave way beneath the vehicle. At first, I was nonplussed. It was only when I opened the driver's door and looked down at a gaping hole, that I understood what had happened. We had been passing over an old, disused latrine, which had been covered over. The weight of the laden Land Cruiser had been too much, and the structure had caved in. But I soon realised that we had been saved from a worse disaster. The solid front bumper bar was resting on the leading edge of the hole, while the back wheels were poised on the rear edge. Had the hole been bigger, the front end of the vehicle would have plunged into it head first, leaving the rear of the vehicle pointing to the sky. We had been very lucky. However, at that moment, I could not see how we were going to extricate the monster. Margarita and I stood transfixed with horror, while the girls howled from the back seat. I could see us telephoning Westlands Motors to break the bad news, and taking the plane back to Nairobi.

But I overlooked the power of human hands and *Harambee,* President Kenyatta's call to pull together. Curiously, this word is from *Hara Ambe,* the Sanskrit reference to the female form of God, *Ambe.* Armed with poles, about twenty men levered that heavy vehicle out of the hole and onto solid ground. I was suitably impressed, and ordered a crate of beer for the rescuers. Of course, it was a great event for them and a lesson for me. It was an experience never to be forgotten.

After leaving the lodge, we set out eastwards through semi-desert, until we reached the treeless expanse of sand that is the Chalbi Desert. It was hot and the sun blazed down, as we followed the sandy track into the wilderness. I had not driven across desert since our drives to the sea in Kuwait. This was unfamiliar country for us, and I felt the thrill I always felt, when faced with nothing but the distant horizon. Eventually, we could see the hills of Marsabit in the distance, and we knew our next destination was not too far off.

Marsabit is a small town that stands on the edge of an extinct volcano. Driving to the top, we found a small lodge, which overlooked a seasonal lake, resting in the bowl of the volcano. The lodge was quiet. I seem to remember having a drink there before finding a place to camp. I forget most of the details of our sojourn there. But I remember the long and tiring journey through monotonous bush country, before we reached Samburu Reserve. I suppose we made a night stop there. We must have been very relieved to get home, with no serious mishap, and satisfied with a memorable safari.

I worked with Westlands Motors for almost three-and-a-half years, until our return to England in May 1976. The Company had dealerships in most of the main towns, one being in Mombasa. Ken Warrilow's young wife was a pilot. One day, I accompanied Ken and the Sales & Marketing Manager on a flying trip to Mombasa, the lady pilot at the controls. It was my first flight in a four-seater, single engine plane. I was relieved to land at Wilson Airport on our return to Nairobi. At the end of his two-year contract, Ken Warrilow left, and his place was taken by Peter Shepherd, who was a Kenya citizen. Peter also had a young wife, Jane, having lost his first wife in an air disaster some years before. Guy Bromley, the Sales Manager, Dick Hedges, the Spare Parts Director, John Gage, the Service Director and Derek Jones, the Service Manager were a friendly team, and meetings were always relaxed. I recently met a Kenyan Indian in Lamu, who was working in D. T. Dobie, just around the corner from Westlands Motors at the same time, and knew several of my colleagues.

John Gage was especially close to us. Unmarried, he lived with his aged mother. One day, after we had returned to the UK, we received news that John had suffered a heart attack and had died. He had moved to Rhodesia, where he had a house. He had often talked enthusiastically about his retirement home, but when he actually made the move, he was unhappy, particularly as his mother had passed away by then. I cried when I received the news of his death.

Nairobi in the 1970's was becoming notorious for armed robbery. The banks were targeted, but offices too. Westlands Motors had its robbery one morning. I was in Peter Shepherd's office, which was at the far end of the corridor from the main entrance, when we heard shots. Peter hurriedly closed and bolted the door of his office. When the robbers had gone, we learnt what had happened. They had entered the main door and fired warning shots, and then pointed a gun at Mr. Jani, the cashier, demanding the money from his till. How did they know where the money was? An inside job perhaps? Mr. Jani received a blow to the head, but apart from that, no one was hurt, but everyone was terrified. The robbers escaped with the contents of the cashbox, a mere few hundred shillings. If they had known the amount of cash on the premises, they would not have risked their lives, for robbery with violence carried the death penalty in Kenya. Later in the day, we had a visit from a journalist from the Standard newspaper. The next day, a picture appeared in the newspaper, showing me pointing at a bullet-hole in the wall. The reader might have thought that I was the hero of the day, tackling armed gangsters single-handed. The truth was, I was hiding in the MD's office!

One morning we got the news, via Mr. Jani, that a Lufthansa Boeing 747 had crashed on taking off from Jomo Kenyatta International Airport in Nairobi, and had burst into flames. The aircraft was carrying one-hundred-and-forty passengers and seventeen crew members. Of these, fifty-five passengers and four crew members died, and there were many injuries. What saddened me most, was to hear that scavengers were actually combing the wreckage of the plane for what they could find of value, even to the extent of removing the possessions from dead bodies. How can people be so heartless?

As Chief Accountant of Westlands Motors, I had my first taste of threatening behaviour from a junior colleague; a supervisor. He often came to work smelling of alcohol, and I warned him many times. Finally, when it was obvious that his drinking habits were interfering with his work, I wrote him a warning letter, and finally dismissed him. He was very nasty, and threatened to have me thrown out of Kenya. I don't believe he could have pulled it off, but nevertheless it was unpleasant.

The first five years in Kenya were happy ones, and all the family managed to stay healthy. My job at Westlands Motors was hardly ever stressful. I would meet the family at Parklands Club often at lunchtime, (Photo No. 27, with Isabel & Cathy by the pool in the sunshine). I would swim forty lengths of the pool, before going back to work in the afternoon. The chlorinated water had no visible effect on my skin, and the exercise was good for my chest, but the downside was the damage the harmful UV rays of the mid-day sun were doing to my skin. I also suffered some bouts of sinusitis, on account of the dryness of the Nairobi climate, but nothing on the scale of the 1960's.

I did visit the doctor periodically for acute bronchitis. An antibiotic was the inevitable treatment. I felt bad about taking time off from my job, so that two days of treatment allowed me to get back to work. It was much later that I understood the folly of this. For many years now, I have avoided antibiotics unless absolutely necessary, and I never take them for bronchitis. I have allowed the body to adjust to a low-level chronic situation. Rarely do I suffer from acute bronchitis, but if I do, I rest and take no antibiotic. It is only recently that my lung capacity has noticeably reduced.

I did have two days in hospital, but that was as the result of an accident. It was my own stupid fault, and I should have known better. It was a typically cold and cloudy Nairobi day in July 1975. It was a Sunday, and we had been to the races at Ngong; the only time I have set foot on a racecourse. Coming back to a cold house late in the afternoon, we decided to light the fire in the sitting room. The wood was damp, and it resisted my repeated attempts to get it going. It appeared to have died completely, so Margarita in her wisdom suggested that a little petrol would help. I should have known not to mess with that highly flammable liquid. I siphoned some from the petrol tank of the car into a jar and sprinkled it on what I thought were lifeless sticks. It ignited with a whoosh. With the shock, I recoiled, spilling petrol on my right hand and arm. My whole arm was soon blazing. The only thing at hand was the sitting room carpet, and I rolled my arm in it. By now, the children had heard the screams and had started to howl. I rushed into the kitchen and held my hand under the cold tap, bringing some relief. It was fortunate that the tough, Indian cotton shirt I was wearing was buttoned up, and covered my wrist and lower arm. Had it not been for that, the burns would have been far worse. It was not clear how badly burnt my right hand was, but when it began to hurt, Margarita wrapped it in a cloth, and drove me to the Aga Khan Hospital casualty wing. There they bathed and bandaged it and gave me some pain killers. That way, I managed to sleep and go to work the next morning, believing that my hand would somehow heal. After two days, it was obvious that it was not going to. I was feeling unwell and in pain. We returned to the hospital. When the nurse removed the bandage, all the skin of my hand came off. At that point, the doctor admitted me. For two days, I was forced to immerse my hand in hot, salty water several times a day. Antibiotics were prescribed, and my hand was left open to the air. After discharge from the hospital, I continued the bathing treatment and wore a light bandage. For several weeks after the new skin grew back, I had to wear a glove. In September, we took a trip to Malawi, Rhodesia and South Africa. The gloved hand can be seen in film of that holiday.

I have very strong memories of that trip to the southern end of Africa in September 1975. It was the only time we ventured out of East Africa during those five years, with the exception of a few days in the Seychelles.

Southern Africa proved to be an eye-opener for me. In the 1970's, South Africa was in the grip of apartheid, the official Government policy of racial segregation, which they euphemistically called 'separate development.' South West Africa was ruled by South Africa, in defiance of the United Nations, and did not become an independent Namibia until 1990. Southern Rhodesia was also ruled by a White Government; Prime Minister, Ian Smith having declared unilateral independence in 1965.

Our first stop was Blantyre, the largest town in Malawi. We stayed a night with the brother of our Kenya friend, Jennifer Collins, and he kindly lent us his Renault, in which we toured the country, driving up the western side of Lake Malawi, (formally Lake Nyasa), through countryside reminiscent of lowland Kenya, with its enormous Baobab trees. The lake is the most southerly of the Great Rift Valley lakes, and the third largest lake in Africa, with a surface area of eleven-thousand square miles (28,500 square kilometres). It is long and narrow, but wide enough to make one believe that one is standing on the beach looking at the ocean.

Next on the itinerary was a short visit to Salisbury, the capital of Rhodesia, renamed Harare when Zimbabwe gained its independence in 1980. In many ways it reminded me of Nairobi when we first landed in 1971. The streets and gardens were full of colour. I wonder what Harare is like today, after the decaying regime of Robert Mugabe, who was president from 1987 until he resigned in 2017.

We flew from there to Johannesburg, the largest and the main industrial city of South Africa. It has an interesting history. The discovery of gold in the 1880's set off a massive influx of prospectors, out of which the City grew rapidly. Johannesburg also has the largest Black African township in Southern Africa. It was in Soweto (an acronym for South West Township) that marches were held in June 1976. Afrikaans had been introduced in racially segregated 'Black' schools, which was widely condemned by that community. The marches led to riots, and many black children were killed by the country's security arm. Even today, despite the introduction of democratic elections in 1994, there is still widespread racial inequality.

Security at that time was good, and we had no fear of walking about. After the abolition of apartheid in 1990, the security situation deteriorated. During a later visit there in 1992, it was not considered safe to be in the streets after dark. We stayed one night in the City-centre but found little of interest there, so we bought tickets for the sleeper train to Durban on the East Natal coast. Durban is a resort town, and an industrial and shipbuilding centre. I remember the lunch that we had in a restaurant on the sea front. It was a cold, wet and windy day. White horses covered the dim sea, and breakers crashed onto the deserted beach. It was September, and the holiday season was still at least two months away. It was no weather for the beach, but we were glad to find a cosy restaurant nearby. We warmed ourselves inside on hot food and wine, while our outsides dried in the warm atmosphere of the dining room.

The next part of our journey was a leisurely drive down the Garden Route to Cape Town. We hired a VW Beetle and set off from Durban. The weather continued cloudy with intermittent rain, as we chugged along, enjoying the freedom that travelling by private car allows. We drove straight through the large town of Port Elizabeth, then made for the little 'White' enclave of Port St. John's, entirely surrounded by the Transkei, the largest of the Bantu Homelands, created by the Apartheid regime to separate Blacks from other races. It was shocking to see the difference, as we crossed from 'White' South Africa into the Transkei, which was arid, and had an aura of poverty. Port St. John's, by contrast, exuded an atmosphere of prosperity. The Transkei was given independence the year after we passed through it. However, this was not recognised outside South Africa. Today, the Bantu Homelands are incorporated into a united South Africa. We must have stayed the night in Port St. John's. I have a vivid memory of standing on the headland overlooking the little sandy bay, and watching the breakers rolling up the beach.

The weather remained wet throughout our drive to Cape Town. We stopped for one night in a Government-owned self-catering cottage. It was very comfortable, with all the facilities one could possibly want. It was a welcome slice of comfort, for the lowering clouds prevented us from experiencing the beaches, or seeing the mountain scenery for which the Garden Route is famous.

The Apartheid policy was evident. Along one stretch of open coastline, we came across a series of signs, indicating which class of people could use which beach. One sign said, 'Blacks only', another, 'Coloureds only', another said, 'Malays only' and the last one, 'Whites only'. Of course, this segregation was enforced in all aspects of daily life, in the use of public toilets, shopping, transport and eating houses. Then there were separate residential areas for the different races. Fortunately, that is all now part of a bad dream. I salute Frederick de Klerk and Nelson Mandela for bringing the hated and diabolical system to an end in the early 1990's, completing the work that de Klerk had started in 1990. They both thoroughly deserved the Nobel Prize that was jointly awarded to them. What a promising year for humanity was 1990! In that year, the Berlin wall, that had been built in 1961 by the East Germans to prevent the fight of East Germans into West Berlin, was demolished, and the City of Berlin was reunited. The collapse of Communism, the disintegration of the Soviet Union and the end of Apartheid occurred at roughly the same time.

Driving through Cape Province on our way to Cape Town, we felt a silent hostility from the Afrikaners. This was in sharp contrast to the hospitality we received that night from people of English stock, as we drove into the little town of Caledon in the pouring rain. We stopped to ask a man if there was a campsite nearby. He brushed our question aside and told us we had to come to his house, as it was no night to be thinking about camping. His wife and two girls, roughly the same age as ours, were at home when we arrived. From the moment we stepped into the warmth and comfort of that house, we were made to feel at home. The wife took charge of our two, bathing them with her own and dressing them in pyjamas. They were given supper, while Margarita and I sat and enjoyed a drink, quite unsure whether to believe what was happening to us. After the children had been put to bed, we four adults had supper together. Then, to crown it all, those wonderful people gave us their own bedroom for the night! We could not have asked for better treatment. It really touched our hearts! And touched mine to this day! The next day, they were involved in a flower show. We were taken along and introduced to the people they met, as friends. Later, we said our goodbyes and thanked them for their loving welcome. We never saw them again. I do not even remember their names. Whatever their opinion about the situation existing in their country, and I believe we did talk about it, I can honestly say that they were wonderful human beings; just the kind to accept with happiness the changes that were to come fifteen years down the line.

Cape Town is a beautiful City, nestling beneath the impressive Table Mountain and hugging Table Bay. It was founded in 1652, and was the first White settlement in Southern Africa. It is the legislative capital of the Country, and a flourishing port. Its distinctive Colonial architecture is famous. I remember two things about Cape Town. The first was the violent wind that we had to battle against, and that almost swept us off our feet. The second was the ascent of Table Mountain in the cable car and the wonderful view of the City from the top. At one point, the car travels almost vertically, giving the occupants a dose of adrenaline. I recorded a film of that exciting rise to the top.

From Cape Town we flew back to Johannesburg, where we picked up the flight back to Nairobi. It had been an interesting and revealing holiday, despite the cold and wet weather.

The other holiday we took outside East Africa was the week we spent in The Seychelles, a group of islands about a thousand kilometres off the east coast of Africa. The main island is Mahe, on which is situated the capital, Victoria. The

Seychelles were taken from the French by the British in 1744. At the time of our visit, The Seychelles had not yet gained its independence; this took place in 1976. In spite of its history of British control, a dialect of French is spoken widely by the inhabitants. Mahe is mountainous, with a narrow coastal strip. The airport, which had only been opened two years before our visit, extends into the Indian Ocean, giving the impression that the plane is coming down in the sea. Before the airport was built, access was only by sea, and for this reason The Seychelles was under-developed as a tourist destination. In fact, we stayed in one of the very few beach hotels. We made a complete circular tour of Mahe one day in a hired car, stopping when we came across a sandy beach. At that time, Victoria was a small town of perhaps twenty-thousand. What I remember of Victoria is the monument in the centre of the town, and the roofs of the buildings, which were almost entirely of corrugated iron sheets in varying shades of rust. Once again, I took a cine film but no photos.

So much activity was crammed into those three years at Westlands Motors. It was fortunate that the job involved hardly any weekend work, which allowed us our weekends free for 'getting away from it all'. One long weekend in October 1974, I made up a party of sixteen, all male friends. Mt. Kenya was the destination, and the conquest of Point Lenana the objective. Batian, the highest peak of Mt. Kenya, is 17,058 ft. above sea level and the second highest mountain in Africa, after Mt. Kilimanjaro. Batian and its sister peak, Nelion, are not for office workers used to lazing beside swimming pools, but for serious climbers, ropes and other equipment being necessary. Nevertheless, Point Lenana is over 16,300 ft., and although no rock climbing is involved, walking uphill at that altitude requires a good deal of stamina and determination.

The climb was arranged through Naro Moru River Lodge, a fishing lodge a few kilometres from the base of the mountain, just off the road from Kiganjo to Nanyuki. The group congregated at the lodge on Friday evening, and early the next morning, we were driven to the Meteorological Station at ten-thousand feet. There began the climb, at first along a good track through a forest, then over open moorland, which was marshy and uneven. But we were lucky, because we carried no backpacks; that was the responsibility of porters, who were used to the altitude. A guide also accompanied us, as often the mist can descend, and the way can easily be lost. Eventually, the ground levelled off, and we started the descent into the deep Teleki Valley, which leads to the permanent tented camp, at the base of the steep climb to the top, (Photo No. 38). The summit is normally shrouded in cloud, except at night and early in the morning. If one is fortunate enough to be there at full moon, the snow-pocked peaks and the glacier present a wonderful sight. We arrived at the camp in the afternoon, giving us a chance to relax and enjoy the warmth of the sun. When the sun dips below the horizon, the temperature plunges rapidly. By the time supper is over, and the climbers crawl into their tents, the ground is beginning to freeze. I was unprepared for a cold night. Even with three bodies in a small space and plenty of clothing, the cold was extreme. After all, we were sleeping at something like fourteen-thousand feet.

We were turned out of our tents at 3.30 in the morning, and provided with a cooked breakfast, eaten in full dress, ready for the final climb to the summit. The reason for the early start was to reach the top of the scree while it was still frozen, it being very difficult to get a foothold when the rock fragments are loose. The other reason was to reach the summit before the cloud descends, and blots out the view from the top.

Goggles and sun screen are important items at high altitudes, especially when walking through snow or across a glacier. Severe sunburn can result if these precautions are not observed. After negotiating the scree, we reached Top Hut, which is used by the mountaineers as a base to scale the rocky peaks. There before us was spread the glacier. We walked along the ridge between it on the left and a sheer drop to the right. At least two members of our party had remained at the tented camp, suffering from mountain sickness or blistered feet. The remaining members can be seen in Photo No. 39, taken by Andrew Little from Top Hut. The figure in the lead, dressed in a light brown jacket, is me. I was feeling fine, if a little breathless, and I was the first to reach the top. There I am, standing on the summit, (Photo No. 40). We rested and admired the splendid view, west across Central Province to the Aberdares, and east towards Meru National Park.

Before long, we were making our way down the mountain, sliding down the scree, and then leaping over the tufts of grass and splashing through the marsh. It took only a short time to reach the Meteorological Station, compared to the uphill climb. Back at the lodge, we changed back into our own clothes and drove back to Nairobi. I guarantee that everyone slept well that night, and for sure, there were some aching limbs in the office the next morning!

As the fifth anniversary of our arrival in Kenya approached, we began to consider the move back to the UK. I had been away far longer than I had planned. I realised that if I was to remain employable I would have to return and enter the commercial world. Kenya had been a wonderful experience. We had seen just about all there was to see from a tourist's point of view. It was time to join the 'real' world again. So, I gave in my notice, and we prepared to return to England. In early 1976, I was thirty-four years old, still young enough to be acceptable to a prospective employer, and with the advantage of having overseas experience. I had no doubt then that I would find employment. Isabel was already seven years old and Cathy just six years. They were at an age where they would be quickly integrated back into English life. The time was ripe for our return.

In the first months of 1976, Kenya suffered a serious drought. We made a trip to Lake Magadi and saw first-hand the effects on the Maasai herds. We passed hundreds of carcasses of cattle and the stench was awful. Milk was in short supply in Nairobi, while butter and cheese were unobtainable. I remember seeing queues of people lining up for maizemeal. At least, at the time I write, the dairy industry is healthy. One finds as much milk, butter and cheese as one could possibly want. In fact, the variety of cheeses now available would have amazed us, had it been on the shelves in 1976. Brown's cheeses, to anyone but an international cheese-taster, are as good as one might find in rural France! But back then, Kenya Cooperative Creameries was a state-owned enterprise, enjoying a virtual monopoly in the dairy industry, resulting in serious shortages of dairy products during dry years.

The Easter weekend of 1976 was spent with the Dobson family in the Arusha National Park, on the slopes of Mt. Kilimanjaro. It was our last safari before our departure. We camped in open heath land with good views. It was the nearest I have ever been to the highest mountain in Africa, a volcanic massif 19,340 ft. high (5,895 metres). Its flat top is permanently covered with snow. During the long rains, snow cover is extensive in the early morning, but this slowly disappears when exposed to the sun. In the hot, dry season, only a small strip if snow can be seen. As time goes on, global warming is eating away at the permanent snow, so that eventually Kilimanjaro will lose its white hair. It is interesting that when the first Europeans beheld Mt. Kilimanjaro, they sent back word that snow existed near the equator. No one believed the story, saying that snow could not possibly survive at that latitude. If they had had access to modern means of communication, they could have sent photographs to the doubters back home, and the matter would have been cleared up. I had no plan to reach the summit. It entails no rock climbing; just a slow plod to the top. The air is rare at 19,000 ft., and putting one foot in front of the other is hard work. I never mustered the enthusiasm for the hike. The Tanzanian Government made the climbers pay a high price, payable only in US dollars! However, I recently took a photo with my mobile phone from the 'safety and comfort' of the passenger seat, on a flight to Mombasa, (Photo No. 41).

What had Kenya given us during those five years? A relaxed and healthy lifestyle certainly. Kenya had shown us a country of enormous variety, scenically and ethnologically. Working alongside Africans and Indians had given me a broader outlook on life. But we had not got to know the indigenous people heart to heart. We had lived an expatriate life, socialising almost exclusively with people of European stock, mostly English and Spanish. Margarita had worked in the Spanish Embassy, gaining valuable experience and showing her administrative skills. Photo No. 42 shows Margarita and I, smartly dressed, in the company of the Spanish Ambassador to Kenya, Sr. Velarde and colleague, Sally. There had been exceptions, such as Peter Kanyago, a trainee accountant, who had worked with me in Cooper Brothers, and whose wedding in Othaya we had attended. And Jane Wanjiru, who became our long-time friend.

Concentrating on our extraordinary five years spent in Kenya, I have to be forgiven for failing to mention our annual visits to Spain. In June 1973, I remember spending some days in Tia Lola's house in Muxia, on Galicia's west coast. John and Cathy joined us there, having taken the bus from La Coruna. We also visited Santiago de Compostela. Two delightful photos taken by John's wife, Cathy, the ace with the camera; one photo of our two girls, Isabel four-years old and Cathy three, (Photo No. 43). In Photo No. 44, John sits with his two nieces.

In the summer of 1974, we were back in Galicia. It was on the 16th August that Jose Luis and Mucha's son, Juan Alberto was christened. Photo No. 45 shows the extended Spanish family, with Mucha's mother holding the baby. It was the year in which Margarita's paternal aunt, Natalia came to Galicia. I have a strong memory of our jolly lunch in the Muxia house, with Tia Natalia commanding at the head of the table. We walked to the church on the hilltop. In Photo No. 46, Isabel and Cathy stand in front of Tia Natalia, another relative from Argentina and Margarita's father, Don Pio, with the sombre church behind. During those years, Isabel and Cathy got to know their Spanish cousins, daughters of my wife's brother, Jose Luis. Margarita and Natalia were one year older than our girls. Photo No. 47 was taken in 1972.

If I had any regrets about my first five years in Kenya, it was not learning to fly an aeroplane. I had a friend, Chris Prior, who was taking a course of flying lessons. Talking with him about the experience I became enthusiastic, and was on the point of booking a course of lessons for myself. Kenya was, at that time, one of the cheapest countries in the World in which to learn to fly. I dallied and, in the end, I failed to make that first move. Perhaps there was that fear of being in control of an aircraft, and at the same time feeling that I was not in control at all. People have said that it is like driving a car: it is just a question of getting used to it. But a car is close to the ground: one only has to stop and get out! Try doing that at ten thousand feet!

It was not the plan, but we were to return to Kenya two years later, in 1978. Although still officially expatriates, we gradually extended our social and working life to include a wide variety of people.

No. 24

No. 25

No. 26

No. 27

No. 28

No. 29

No. 30

No. 31

No. 32

No. 33

No. 34

No. 35

No. 36

No. 37

No. 38

No. 39

No. 40

No. 41

No. 42

No. 43

No. 44

No. 45

No. 46

No. 47

BACK IN THE UK

1976-1978

THE ENGLISH SUMMER OF 1976 WAS the hottest and driest I can remember. In fact, we are told that it was the driest summer since 1727. We arrived back in England in the middle of May to warm spring weather. Photo No. 48, taken in a bone-dry London park, a short time after our arrival back in England, is evidence for this.

Summer comes to the Mediterranean countries earlier than it does further north. We had taken an Olympic Airways flight to Athens and checked into a hotel there, courtesy of Olympic. The days were hot and sunny and the nights refreshingly cool. By contrast, the sea was cold enough to set our bodies aching. Water takes far longer to warm up than the land. I believe we stayed in Greece for two nights, but the only clear memory is the boat trip we took to the Island of Hydra. It was a fairly large vessel. We steamed out of the port and past coastal villages, the passengers lining the guard rail. There was plenty to see from the deck. Hydra itself was about a three-hour cruise. The little fishing village, perhaps the main settlement on the island, was our port of call. We went ashore and wandered the little streets between pretty, whitewashed houses, all crowded around the harbour. We must have had lunch there, although I neither remember the place nor the food we ate. But we did have a dip in the cold sea. Back in Athens, we did other touristy things, like visiting the Acropolis and the Parthenon; a must for any visitors to Athens, before flying out to London.

I had decided to take a long break from work, to spend the summer months relaxing and travelling. For this purpose, we decided to look for a camper van, like the one we had in Kenya, which gave us so much pleasure. So, after a few days winding down, we went looking for a suitable second-hand camper. Before long, we saw a Bedford Dormobile in a second-hand dealer at £1,800: a reasonable price. It turned out to be a wonderful buy, never giving us a moment's anxiety. There was sleeping space for Margarita and me, created from the bench seats, and bunks high up on either side for the children as well. Cooking was by gas, and there was cupboard space too. Could there have been a fridge? Anyway, the internal arrangements were convenient. We parked the Bedford in the back garden of Yew Cottage, and there we slept whenever we were staying with my parents. It was good for Mum and Dad to have their two granddaughters, who got to know their young cousins, Paul and Claire too. Photo No. 49, (one of my favourites), shows a proud grandpa, wheeling his four small grandchildren around the garden of Yew Cottage in that summer of 1976. And we could not have asked for a more perfect summer!

My sister, Jean and husband, Richard had been married for five years. They had lived for a time in Woodcote, north of Reading, before moving to Minster Lovell, on the far side of Oxford. My brother, John had already married Catherine Walker in the summer of 1972. Soon after, they bought a little semi-detached house in Clairville Gardens, in the north-east London suburb of Hanwell. John, being an architect, proceeded to improve the house. He writes, and I quote, 'We bought our house in Clairville Gardens in 1972, not long before we were married. It was built in 1890, probably without a bathroom, but a crude one had been fitted within one end of the kitchen. Cathy took a photo of it shortly after we moved in, before we started renovations, and this hung on the wall for many years to remind us of just how grotty it was, and how far we had come. We relocated the bath/toilet upstairs in one of the three bedrooms, and extended the kitchen to occupy the void.' John and Cathy kept the house for some years after moving to Auckland in New Zealand in 1979, but finally sold it when they decided to make New Zealand their permanent home.

Soon after our return from Kenya, we drove down to Bath, to inspect the house where we had lived up to December 1970, when we had put it in the hands of a local letting agent. The tenants had recently moved out and had left the house in a poor state. We set about the job of cleaning throughout. The kitchen cooker was in a disgusting condition. It made us quite sick to see it. When we were satisfied with our work, we put the house on the market, and returned to our temporary home in the Bedford Dormobile. Our idea was to buy a better house nearer to my parents, now that we had saved some money. Margarita had worked at the Spanish Embassy in Nairobi for most of the five years, and we had managed to build up a reasonable balance in a savings account.

Meanwhile, our family of four continued to enjoy the wonderful weather and the freedom of movement. We visited friends we had made in Nairobi, and who had already moved back to England. We went to Bournemouth one weekend, and sat on the beach in the hot sun. It was immediately after that weekend that I came out in red spots all over my back. I went to see the skin specialist in The Royal Berkshire Hospital in Reading. He asked me about my lifestyle. When I told him, he said in no uncertain language that I had ruined my skin by exposing it year after year to the tropical sun. It was the beginning of my fight with skin cancer, which still affects me today, nearly fifty years later.

With another ex-Kenya couple, Tony and Carole Fletcher, we flew to Tunisia for a week, staying in a resort hotel in the south of the country. I remember a trip by bus to Tunis, the stroll through the bazaar and the ruins of Carthage. In contrast, I also remember something extremely trivial; the waiter coming around the breakfast room with oranges, announcing the fact in French. Another day, the hotel organised a swimming competition, which I entered.

One of the main reasons for buying the camper van was to tour Spain that autumn, before settling down to a full-time job. We had been to Spain every year since getting married, but I had never explored the country, with the exception of the Region of Galicia, and the road from France across the northern coast to La Coruna. Spain is incredibly rich in diversity of scenery and cultures, and divided into seventeen autonomous regions. It was time I got to know it.

The ancient kingdoms of Castilla and Aragon had united in 1469, following the marriage of Isabella I and Ferdinand, rulers of the two states. During their joint rule, they expelled the Jews and the Moors from Spain and unified the Country. They financed Columbus' voyage of discovery, and the new united Spain became a great European power, rivalling England for mastery of the seas, and in the process, acquiring many overseas possessions, especially in America. Following the loss of their empire in the 19th Century, Spain ceased to be a world power, and in fact became one of the poorest countries in Western Europe. In 1931, King Alfonso XIII abdicated, and Spain became a republic. Following the savage Spanish civil war of 1936 to 1939, in which over a million Spaniards died, General Francisco Franco, the leader of the Falangists, who had defeated the Republicans, established a dictatorship, which was to last until his death in 1975. Before he died, he named Juan Carlos, the grandson of Alfonso, as King of Spain. At the time of our 1976 tour of Spain, the monarchy had been established once more, but the Country was only beginning to recover from thirty-six years of relative isolation and economic stagnation. Today, Following the abdication of Juan Carlos, his son, Felipe VI rules as a figurehead, bringing progress to a growing industrial democracy. Spain is today a committed member of the European Union, using the Euro currency, and the fourth largest economy in the Euro zone, as well as the sixteenth largest world economy.

It was September when we left England in the Bedford for our Spanish tour. We crossed the English Channel by ferry and drove across France, following the same route that John and I had taken almost exactly ten years earlier. I seem to remember we took a different route across Northern Spain to La Coruna. Some advances had been made in the quality of roads since our earlier trip. We stayed a few days with Margarita's family in La Coruna, before heading southwards, leaving the girls with their *abuelito*.

The Bedford was a comfortable car to drive, once I had got used to the width of it. The driving seat was high, giving the driver a clear view out of the front windscreen. I had no trouble with driving on the right-hand side of the road, except that I needed Margarita's help when overtaking another vehicle. But speed was not my aim. I think the only vehicles I overtook were the horse-drawn kind; perhaps the odd laden lorry too! We had weeks ahead of us and we were in no hurry. We plotted our way on a roadmap of Spain.

Galicia is a mountainous Region, cut off from the rest of Spain by a range of mountains, which in winter can often be snowbound. It is closer geographically and ethnologically to Portugal, its southern neighbour, and in fact the regional language, *gallego*, shares the same ancestry as Portuguese. The natives of Galicia are Celts, and share many characteristics with the Irish, the Welsh and the Bretons. Galicia is divided into four *provincias*, La Coruna, Lugo, Orense and Pontevedra.

Rural Spain at that time saw few tourists, and a parked camper van with curtains drawn across raised no eyebrows. We were therefore able to pull up and sleep wherever and whenever it was convenient, even in the centre of the town. This we often did. The first night after leaving La Coruna was spent in Orense, and the following day we crossed the mountains into the Province of Zamora, which is dry and the soil is red. It could not have been more of a contrast. The small town of the same name seemed to be built of the same red soil. We stopped for the next night in Salamanca, an ancient city with a large university and a long cultural history. Here we turned the snub nose of the Bedford eastwards towards Central Spain, climbing up onto the central plateau. We spent two or three days exploring the ancient towns of Avila and Segovia, both steeped in history. The old part of Avila is still ringed by an 11th Century wall, and in the centre stands a Romanesque cathedral. In Segovia we saw the famous Roman aqueduct, soaring above the city.

From there, we continued our journey south-westwards, following the long *El Rio Tajo* valley, down into one of the most beautiful parts of Spain; the region of Extremadura, and the pretty town of Caceres. As we drove south, the weather became warmer and the vegetation more luxuriant. After the towns of Badajoz and Zafra, the road descends onto the plains of Huelva. The town of Huelva was uninteresting. The only thing I remember was going into a call box and phoning Isabel and Cathy. I do believe they were having a great time and, for sure, Lolita, their *Madrina,* was enjoying spoiling them! Much of the province of Huelva is flat and marshy, and its wetlands hold an important habitat for birdlife. What spoilt the area for me was the presence of an ugly Rio Tinto Zinc chemical factory, which spewed out noxious fumes.

We then crossed into Andalucia; the most southern region of Spain. It is famous, among other things, for its olives and its 'White Towns' and villages, perched on top of hills, or clinging precariously to steep hillsides. The visual effect, from far across the valley, is like a pile of pure white stones. White reflects the light and heat, an important consideration in summer, when the temperature can rise into the forties centigrade. The roofs of the houses are something between soft light brown, slightly red or orange, but with an overall grey appearance. The total effect is one that pleases the eye. The streets of these towns and villages are mostly narrow. On more than one occasion, we wondered if the Bedford would squeeze through between the houses on each side of the street. Once, I had to back up, the street of one village being too narrow for our car to pass.

Andalucia is the home of *Flamenco* music and dance, brought by the Gypsies, who settled in the region some centuries ago. Like the Gypsies throughout Europe, they continue a nomadic life, although while we were in Granada, we noticed that they inhabit caves in the hillsides around the City. In Spain, the *Gitanos* are generally disliked, due to their perceived dishonesty and their aggressive begging behaviour.

The port city of Cadiz was the home of the parents of Margarita's cousin, Tere. They passed away years ago but many of her family live there today. At the time of our visit in 1976, Tere's mother was still alive. Margarita and I were entertained by the family, and it was a welcome break from travelling. Cadiz is a lively city, full of bars. I remember the sumptuous *tapas,* served with the local *vino*. Not far from Cadiz, is the town of *Jerez,* the name given also to the fortified wine, popular throughout the World under the English name 'Sherry.' Brandy is also produced in the area. Cadiz was a Phoenician trading colony as early as 1100 AD, and later became a major port for trade with America. In 1805, it was from Cadiz that the Spanish fleet sailed to engage Nelson's fleet at the Battle of Trafalgar.

Motoring eastwards, we took the coast road. Standing on the cliff one day, we looked across the Mediterranean to the north coast of Africa, only a few kilometres away. We spent a night in the Bedford close by, parked overlooking the beach. The next day saw us driving along *La Costa del Sol* of Malaga, through such resorts as Puerto Banus, Marbella and Torremolinos. We have been back to that area so often in later years. I know that we stayed in the beautiful City of Granada, the former Moorish capital of the Kingdom of that name. Perhaps Granada's most exquisite legacy of the Muslim Moors, who ruled Andalucia for seven-hundred years, is the Alhambra Palace, built in the 13th and 14th Centuries. The palace, together with its gardens, is one of the most popular tourist attractions in Spain.

From Granada we drove north, stopping at Toledo, before finally reaching Madrid, where we were to be reunited with our children. What had Margarita and I talked about during those many hours together, sitting in the front seats of the Bedford? We would have commented on and discussed the places we were seeing, and she would have told me what she knew about the different cultures and customs of those places. We passed through the part of Granada where her father had been held in a concentration camp at the end of the Civil War. Luckily, he was a qualified doctor, and was considered useful to the Nationalists. But his wife would half expect every day to be told that he had been executed. But he survived his imprisonment. Their son, Jose Luis, was born in a village in Granada, in 1938.

Jose lived in an apartment complex on the outskirts of Madrid with his wife, Mucha and his two girls, Margarita and Natalia. On our return from the tour, we stayed with them, perhaps for a few days, before packing up the Dormobile and driving back home. It must have been October by then, and cooling off. Madrid can be very cold in the winter, situated in the centre of the Iberian Peninsula, and high on the *meseta* as it is. We took the road to Zaragoza, and then north through Lerida to the Pyrenees, the range of mountains that divide Spain from France. That route took us through the Principality of Andorra. The mountains were already covered with snow. We drove through a snow storm, before descending into France, and to the city of Toulouse. The drive north from there was exceptionally beautiful. I clearly remember stopping on the road one afternoon, and enjoying the warmth of the autumn sun. I can see it now, with the help of a lost photo, with the back door of the van open, revealing the strings of onions and garlic that we had brought from Spain. A case of *rioja* was also on board, and we hoped the English customs would allow us through.

Eventually, we arrived back in England, having covered more than six thousand kilometres, without so much as a puncture. The car had behaved perfectly, and had saved us a fortune in hotel bills to boot!

By that time, autumn was well under way, and we needed to get the girls into school. We had to move house, and I needed to earn some money to feed the family through the winter. There was a lot to do but it went well. We sold our house in Bath for £11,000. The value had increased by 240 percent in seven-and-a-half years. If we had been daring in 1968 and had bought that detached house with the orchard, what kind of profit would we have made? But we had not done it, and there was no use regretting the decision. We had benefitted from a period of high inflation and would continue to benefit, as the rise in house prices showed no sign of abating.

We bought a fairly new terraced town house in the pretty village of Whitchurch, surrounded by beech woods, just over the toll bridge from Pangbourne, and about five miles from Upper Basildon. No. 21, Hillside was on three levels. The front door opened onto a hallway, behind which was a small room. There was a garage for the car. The stairs led to the sitting/dining room and a small kitchen. The back door led onto a patio backed by woods, sloping steeply up the hill. Upstairs were three bedrooms and a bathroom. The previous owners left us good quality carpets in excellent condition, included in the £21,000 we paid. I took out an endowment mortgage of £7,000 and settled the rest from our savings. So far so good!

The village school, only a few minutes' walk from the house, was informal and friendly under the headmastership of Mr. Loveday. The girls, now seven and six years old, soon settled in. We made friends in Hillside. Living next door but one was a young couple; Gina and Roger Goodall. She was a native of Birmingham, a down-to-earth, straight talker, with the accent to go with it. Roger was rather quieter. We spent a lot of time together. A few years later, on a visit to Hillside, we met Gina, who was still living in the house. She surprised us by telling us that Roger had one day just left, leaving behind a note of farewell. According to her story, he had gone off to live with another man. He had never told her of his inclinations to homosexuality. It must have given her a shock. She had lived with him for several years and she had obviously not known him well. Gina attended Christopher's Christening in 1984.

Isabel became friends with a little girl called Imogen, living a few doors away. Her mother was the daughter of Laurence Olivier, the famous actor. I remember that she had lit a fire in the grate in her sitting room, and nearly burnt the house down. We discovered from that incident that the fireplaces of all the houses in the row were put straight onto wooden floor joists! We had not been told this by the previous owners, and it was as well we never lit a fire in the grate.

Our sitting room faced the quiet cul-de-sac and an enormous beech tree. In winter it was bare, in spring a mass of light green, in summer a thick, mature green and in autumn a blend of reds, browns, oranges and yellows. The winds of autumn would shake the tree, and down would come the leaves, floating, twirling and falling, to lay a multi-coloured carpet ankle deep, in the road and in the front gardens. Several times in that season, a weekend would find us sweeping leaves. In Photo No. 53, Isabel and Imogen sweep, while Margarita and Cathy stand in front of the Dormobile. Nature's rhythm was repeated throughout the neighbouring beech woods, including our patio behind the house. In rainy weather the carpet could become slippery.

Dad came over to help us redecorate the hall and to hang new wallpaper. The house had been occupied by a middle-aged couple without children, and was in excellent condition. My parents were frequent visitors. The only bone of contention was their attachment to their two Golden Retriever dogs, which we preferred to remain downstairs in the hall, rather than spread themselves and their hairs on the sitting room carpet, particularly in wet weather.

Before long, I was scanning the job advertisements in the newspapers and writing application letters. After some time, when I saw no results, I got demoralised. I had signed on as unemployed and received a weekly unemployment benefit, which was not a great deal, but it helped to pay the expenses. Meanwhile, Margarita had become an Avon sales representative, knocking on front doors to sell cosmetics. It was hard work, but Margarita was not one to give up and she persevered for some time. Then she got the chance of becoming a Tupperware dealer. She was a sociable person, and soon organised her evening parties, at which the different products were demonstrated, and invitees were persuaded to buy. Tupperware was a quality product with a long and effective life. The Company policy was only to give a commission on sales to the dealers, managers and distributors. Prizes are also awarded to high achievers. The distributor for our area was a young, dynamic couple. They soon saw Margarita's potential. She became a manager, which meant she had to recruit, train and encourage a group of dealers, who would hold parties, at which Margarita would often attend. For this she earned a commission on all the sales of her group. And she was given a Company car as well. It was the promise of a car that spurred her into achieving managerial status. She was often at the top of the sales lists. Every Monday morning, the distributors would have a sales meeting. We used to laugh about the song they used to play, whenever a high selling manager or dealer was praised. It was the song, 'Isn't she lovely? Isn't she wonderful?'

Unemployment benefits were not paid out indefinitely. I had to accept to be interviewed for a job, even if it was one I was not really interested in, or lose the benefit. A temporary assignment came up with a rapidly growing telecommunication company, Racal Engineering, with offices on the south side of Reading. The pay was reasonable, so much per hour for the hours worked in the week. The work involved writing up cash books (the normal manner of bookkeeping at that time). I had no responsibility whatever outside that task. It was easy, but after some time, monotonous. It certainly was not work that I had spent years training for and for which I had become a Chartered Accountant. I saw management staff around me, who were not even qualified, and I felt that I was wasting my time, but I continued working at Racal, driving there and back in the Bedford.

Margarita's job meant most evenings out attending Tupperware parties. I was becoming depressed. I would sit at home and listen to music, or watch television and drink homemade beer. I felt guilty that Margarita was slaving hard and also managing the house. I did help where I could, but perhaps not as much as I should have done.

Eventually, in February 1978, a situation became vacant for a financial accountant at Reading Newspapers Limited, and I got the job. It entailed supervision of the accounts department and preparation of monthly management accounts, budgets and other financial reports. I did not enjoy it in the least. The accounts department was staffed by a bunch of middle-aged dragons, who were in the habit of eating young accountants for lunch! I was supposed to supervise them, but were they about to listen to a newly employed young man, when they had been there for donkey's years and knew their jobs? I spent my lunch hour walking around Reading, and my day watching the clock for going-home time. It was a relief to get off the train in Pangbourne and walk home up the hill. I suppose I could have got used to the job, and perhaps in time I may even have enjoyed it, and maybe even get promotion. But something happened to change all that.

It must have been January of 1978 that I saw an advertisement for a Chief Accountant with the Mercat Group in Nairobi. As a matter of interest, I sent off a reply with my latest CV. It was not my intention to return to Kenya at that time, but I applied for the job just the same. Then I promptly forgot about it. The weeks passed, and the job at Reading Newspapers had come along. It was not until at least two months after this, that I received a telephone call from London out of the blue. The caller introduced himself as the Finance Director of Mercat. At first, I did not understand why he was calling me. When he told me that he was in London to conduct interviews for the job in

Nairobi, I remembered my application letter. Now I was in a fix! I had a permanent job; not the best in the world but a job nonetheless. I told him that I was now employed and not interested in going back to Kenya. But he was clever! He said that even if I were not interested, I should meet him in London, and he would pay all the expenses, and there was no commitment on my part. Well why not? I took the train to London and met him, Bob 'something or other.' He said I was number one on the list for the job, due to my qualifications, professional experience and Kenya experience in a similar position. The terms were attractive. I told him that I would talk to my wife and call him in a day or two.

On the way home, I began to get excited about the idea of going back to Kenya, where we had been so happy. The Reading job was a bore, and I was doubting the likelihood of getting back on a good level in commerce in England. It took very little discussion that evening before we decided to give it a go. Margarita found the English climate unfriendly, especially the long winter months. This time, it would be a long term move. I telephoned Bob and accepted the job. From that time, all I could think of was going back to Nairobi. Of course, my parents were disappointed. They were getting used to having us nearby. It was a double blow, when John and Cathy decided to move to New Zealand in February of the following year. The Managing Director of Reading Newspapers was not happy either, when I handed in my three months' notice. I had worked there for a bare three months. When I think about Bob's persuasion; his smart way of attracting me to meet him, I ask myself what would have been our future; not only mine but children and grandchildren too, had I not travelled to London for that interview!

During those three months, before I departed for Africa, Cathy's Christening was held. We had decided not to perform the ceremony until she was old enough to decide for herself. At the time of the Christening, Mum and Dad were still enjoying Yew Cottage. Tia Tere was present at the Christening, as well as cousins, Margarita and Natalia, who came over from Spain, (Photo No. 50, with Tia Tere), and (No. 51, with Margarita and Natalia). A delightful photo of Margarita was taken on the same day, (Photo No. 52).

So, we set about preparing to move once more to Africa. Dudley Singleton was to let 21, Hillside after our departure. This arrangement lasted a few years, after which my father took over the letting, earning himself some extra money for it. This time, we had more possessions than would fit in a trunk, like the one that had sailed to Kenya via Barbados. I expect we flew to Spain to see Margarita's father that summer, as we had done every year since getting married.

RETURN TO KENYA

Working with Elliot's Bakeries

IT WAS DECIDED THAT I would fly to Nairobi at the end of July to sort out the accommodation, before Margarita followed with the children. I arrived in Nairobi around the 27th July 1978, and went to stay with Anne and Phil Dobson in Muthangari Close in Lavington.

Elliot's Bakeries Limited was the largest producer of factory-made bread in Kenya in 1978. In fact, bread was not baked on a large scale in Kenya at the time of our first five- year tour. We had bought our bread from the Oven Door Bakery in Westlands. Up-country Africans still considered *ugali* (maize meal cake) their staple food. For the Kikuyu, it was also *irio* and *githeri,* both made with whole maize. For people of the coast, rice was, and still is, the staple food. Bread was the food of the White people, and some well-to-do Africans. With the rise of the middle class, Kenyans began to eat bread. Today, white bread is consumed in large quantities, even by the lower paid, a fact that I think is detrimental to general health. But brown bread consumption is increasing. By the late 1970's, competitors were appearing on the scene, eager to take advantage of the ballooning market. Elliot's' marketing function was virtually non-existent; its position as the leader in the market taken for granted. Slowly, that position was eroded. Added to that, the senior management of the Company was involved in negligence and corruption.

It was against this background that I took over the job from the former Chief Accountant, Ian McEwen, who, together with the General Manager and the Marketing Manager, had been relieved of their responsibilities. Some years ago, I met someone who knew Ian well, and he told me that Ian had died of alcoholism. On my first day at work, Bob took me to the Elliot's' premises in Changamwe Road, in the Industrial Area of Nairobi. We spent the day going through the books and the latest Audited Accounts. It was then that I realised what a job was in store for me! A long list of bad debts would have to be written off, and the internal control systems reviewed. The results for the year would show a big loss, and I was the one to prepare those accounts. The new General Manager was a Pakistani by the name Qureshi. Had he been a dynamic leader instead of a wishy-washy man, Elliot's might have increased its production in line with rising market volume. But he was not, and he allowed a tiny marketing department to bumble along. The Company was bound to do well in the short term, because the demand for bread was there. So, we made increasing profits in the three years I was there. The financial and production controls were put into place. However, some years later, Elliot's went into receivership, although today it still bakes bread, holding a very miniscule share of the market.

The house we were allocated was in School Lane, Westlands. It was a detached, stone bungalow, with a large, attractive back garden and a front drive set in flower gardens. The kitchen was small, but we later talked with the Chairman, Jack Jones, and he saw the sense in creating a modern kitchen: it would add value to the house. We were very pleased with the result.

Margarita and the girls arrived about the 10th August, and the house was ready for us. No sooner had we settled in, when the Country was rocked by the news of the death of President Kenyatta while at his Mombasa home. It was the 22nd August. Rumours were flying around Nairobi that there was going to be serious trouble. This was because, under the Kenyan Constitution, the Vice-President automatically succeeded to the Presidency on the death of the incumbent, until elections were held. There was a clique of Kikuyu politicians who wanted to stop Vice-President Daniel arap Moi from becoming President. Moi was a member of the Kalenjin group of tribes. This Kikuyu clique was grooming Mbiyu Koinange, Kenyatta's son-in-law, for the post. In fact, there had been a move to change the Constitution some years earlier, but it had not succeeded. As it happened, Moi had some influential supporters who knew of the plot. The Vice-President was whisked away from Nairobi and quickly sworn in as President, so thwarting the plan. We decided, together with other friends, to take a few days at the coast, to wait for the situation to cool down. From Nyali Beach Hotel, we followed the news with interest. In the event, there was no trouble. Over the years, Moi strengthened his grip on power. He ruled Kenya with an iron hand for twenty-four years, before he was defeated in multi-party elections in 2002.

One of the first concerns on arrival in Kenya was to find a suitable school for Isabel, now approaching her tenth birthday, and Cathy, eight years. Isabel had attended Loreto Convent in Valley Road in the year before we returned to England, but we discarded that school. There were the up-market Nairobi preparatory schools but they were expensive. In the end, we decided on Imani School in Thika. It meant boarding during the week and coming home for weekends. We thought the girls were ready for that. The school was opening a hostel a couple of kilometres away, to be run by a European couple, Mr and Mrs Irwin. The hostel was not finished when we went to view it, but it occupied a wonderful position by a dam in the middle of a coffee plantation. After the girls left the school, the hostel was closed, and the boarding house was brought into the school premises for security reasons. Security was becoming a serious issue in Kenya, and perhaps the move was timely. However, the girls had some wild times in the hostel. How they did not contract bilharzia from swimming in the dam, I don't know! Mrs Irwin was very strict. Isabel still remembers how Mrs Irwin would force her to finish her plate of macaroni, which Isabel declared was inedible.

The school itself had been built to cater for the children of senior employees of Kenya Canners Limited, the owners of the pineapple plantation, which covered many square miles of the surrounding area. In 1978, the school was opened to children from outside. Many White Kenyan families sent their children there. In this way, our girls made friends with many children of citizen families. They are still in touch with some of the friends they made at Imani School.

Now that I was working in the baking industry, rather than the motor industry, our *kali* safaris were curtailed. It is not true to say that we stayed at home. We did many trips, to the National Parks, to the coast and to a private ranch, but Elliot's had allocated a Renault 16 for my use, and it was not ideal for safaris into the bush. But we developed other interests.

We became members of the Donovan Maule Theatre Club. It was an excellent theatre, under the direction of James Falkland, and with professional actors of the class of Kenneth Mason and James Ward. Every three weeks a new play would be staged; those selected from the rich repertoire of English language plays by the great playwrights. We hardly missed a performance. When the DM Theatre was demolished, the theatre group moved to the newly-opened Professional Centre across the road, occupying the basement. The stage was very small and the auditorium held some two hundred seats. Sitting in the front row, the spectators were almost within reach of the actors, which brought the action so close that one almost felt part of it. This intimacy we found appealing. Gradually, more and more African players joined, and the group put on some plays with an African flavour, so that the club began to attract a wider audience.

It was on our return to Kenya in 1978 that I began to develop some of my creative skills, and began to take an interest in poetry and literature. A short time after our arrival, I had a very strong urge to try my hand at painting. I bought an artist's pad, and a set of water colour paints. It was during the Christmas holidays of that year that I put brush to paper for the first time. We had rented two cottages in a small development in Malindi, one for us and one for the Dobsons; Anne, Phil, Caroline and baby Mark. I was not happy with my first attempt at the art, so in 1979, when I got to hear of an art teacher by the name of Dora Betts, I called her. Mrs Betts had been an active member of the local Art Society for twenty-five years. I took lessons from her for about nine months. She set me on the road, and I am grateful to her. She told me very clearly that she couldn't teach me how to paint, but she could show me some basic techniques, after which it was for me to develop my style as I practiced. It proved to be true. As the months passed, I became more confident, and was pleased with the work I was doing. Mrs. Betts must have been a widow or unmarried. She was a funny old stick! I went twice a week to her house off Ngong Road. She used to sit beside me, chain-smoking, while I painted. She had a rough cough, typical of a heavy smoker. She also loved her brandy. She would have loved to drink Cognac but couldn't afford to, so she had to be content with the locally distilled one, which she contemptuously denounced as 'Cat's pee!'

Once I had collected a number of watercolour paintings, chiefly landscapes and street scenes, I decided to hold an exhibition. It was in 1980 or 1981. The Donovan Maule Theatre allowed me to display them on the walls of the foyer in exchange for a commission. It was a very successful exhibition, at which I sold a number of paintings, and this spurred me on. At that time, we lived in School Lane. An extension had been added to the girls' bedroom, and it was in that room that I spent much of my spare time. Doing a painting took a lot of energy, but once I had started on one, I did not want to be interrupted, even for meals!

I remember one morning, while sitting at my painting table, when I received a telephone call from Elliot's, to say there had been an armed robbery at the factory and a large amount of money had been stolen. One of the security guards had been killed. The robbers must have known the money was there; tipped off by someone on the inside perhaps. It was a weekday, because I was alone in the house, possibly having a day off work. The girls were at school and Margarita was at work. She was at that time working at the Colombian Embassy. I was not expected to rush to the factory: I was just being informed. But I panicked! Why? Because I had been thinking of reviewing the insured amounts stated in our various insurance policies, but had been putting it off. Now I was terrified that we were not adequately covered for loss of cash, and I would face the music. The only thing I could think of doing was to get the brandy bottle out, and take a very large measure to try to regain my composure. The first thing I did, when returning to the office, was to take out the file and check on the sum assured for theft of cash. The claim must have been settled, because nothing more was ever said about it. But I had an extremely worrying few hours.

At that time, Margarita worked as the secretary to the Ambassador of Colombia, with the office and residence at the end of Muthaiga Road. The Ambassador, Dr. Guillermo Nanetti Concha, had been the Minister of Education in his country, but had fallen in love with his young secretary, Gloria, who was related to the President. He had asked for a diplomatic post abroad to escape a scandal, taking Gloria with him, and leaving his wife and children behind. Gloria had no passport of her own, but was included in his. She often complained to Margarita that she was given no money. The Ambassador's treatment of his companion was indicative of his miserly nature, which also showed itself by expecting Margarita to use her personal car for Embassy business with insufficient compensation. The Automobile Association has two rates; one with and one without insurance. He paid her the rate without insurance. In other ways he was a good employer. He was a very cultured man, and Margarita got on well with him. He respected her and sometimes confided in her. When he was dying of cancer of the stomach and was confined to bed, he would call her to his room and talk to her. He also liked and respected me.

Gloria saw herself almost as a Goddess, so much so that she had grown up wondering why she had to go to the toilet like ordinary mortals. She was fussy in the extreme, going to the lengths of measuring the distance between the individual pieces of cutlery when setting the table for dinner guests, just to make sure the table was perfect. She feared Dr. Nanetti's death, because he had never married her, and she had no passport. But on his deathbed, he did have a ceremony performed, in which she formally became Mrs Nanetti. After his death, she went to Spain and married a bullfighter; an ideal end to a strange story!

With Margarita's job in the Embassy of a Latin country, we were back in the Spanish-speaking society of Nairobi. About that time, the Mexican Government opened an Embassy. We became friends with the diplomat who had been sent to establish the Mission; Jaime Cordero. The Mexican

Government had bought a plot in Loresho, and were building an office and a residence for the Ambassador, who was yet to arrive. Jaime lived with a companion, Hector Piccini, as well as his mother and an aunt. When the Embassy opened and the full staff arrived, we were invited to many functions; dinners, lunches and parties, and our house was the scene of many social gatherings. The Ambassador, Enrique Buj, was a big, fat man with a big fat appetite for wine. When in our School Lane house for lunch, he would deplete our wine stocks, which was fine, since the stocks came from the embassy duty free. He would always bring to our house his own large, green, plastic mug, which would need to be kept topped up. He was a very jovial man, as can be seen in Photo No. 54, taken in 1984, with Margarita and I and his wife, suitably dressed. Other friends from the Embassy were Benito Andion, Hector Raul Acosta and Alejandro Ortiz. Of the three, only Benito was married. The others were undoubtedly gay, including Jaime and Hector, although the matter was never discussed. Photo No. 55, taken in the back garden of the School Lane house in December 1979, manifests the Spanish influence.

During this time, the Spanish Embassy arranged for the visit to Kenya of *La Tuna de Malaga*. Universities in Spain have a band that plays popular and traditional Spanish songs. We had the pleasure of hosting a lunch party for some of them at our School Lane house, to which the Mexicans were also invited. It was a memorable afternoon. We bought a gramophone record from them of some of their best-known songs.

Most of our friends during those times were Spanish-speaking, thanks to Margarita's sociable nature. But she became good friends with a Kikuyu girl, Jane Wanjiru. Jane had been married, but the husband had been killed in a road accident, leaving her with three young children. His family came and removed everything from her house after the funeral, including some of the children's clothes, apparently a common strategy in their culture, but one that is very alien to our ideas of fair play. She struggled to bring them up and educate them with her earnings as a masseuse and a beautician. In a later Photo, No. 56, we see her massaging Christopher. Her children, Njoroge, Mary and Grace, were older than our girls. Later, when her children had grown up, Jane went to work in Scotland, and there she met and married Steve, a Scotsman, who owned a boat workshop. They lived in Scotland, but they regularly took an annual holiday in Nairobi, during which they could usually be found beside the pool at Parklands Sports Club, entertaining members of Jane's extended family. One year, the couple visited us at my parents' house in Theale, (Photo No. 57). She was loved by their Scottish friends. She recently passed away in Scotland.

We made other friends through our membership of Parklands Sports Club, which we had been lucky to renew on our return to Kenya. We had given up our membership in 1976, not imagining that we would come back in two years. But the chairmanship of the club had not changed in the intervening time, and Norrie Shapira just allowed us back in, just as if we had never been away! Norrie's position was like that of benign dictator, and nobody would have thought of questioning his decision. He had been chairman for years. I can draw a parallel between Norrie and President Moi, who became a benign dictator, with perhaps some tendencies to malignancy, and ruled Kenya for twenty-four years. The time for dictatorships has now passed, at club level and at National level too, but in 1978, the club atmosphere was very relaxed. For example, we used to bring a picnic and eat it on the grass within the swimming pool area. Now, there is no grass to sit on: tables and chairs occupy most of the available space, notices prohibit smoking and the use of mobile phones and one cannot bring food from outside. I have heard the odd complaint that the club has the atmosphere of a hotel. On the other hand, the facilities are extensive and the service of good quality. One cannot have one's cake and eat it too!

One of our favourite coastal lodges at that time was the Driftwood Club, situated on Casuarina Beach in Malindi. It consisted of about ten little thatched cottages, arranged around a restaurant and a bar. There was a swimming pool, and the beach was adjacent. It was the haunt of many White Kenyans. What endeared the place to us was its casual atmosphere. There was no dress code and children could come and go anywhere, even to the bar. One year, we spent Christmas there, and it rained cats and dogs the whole time. At one time, the Manager was Steve Nicholas, the brother of Sally, the classical blonde English girl with whom Margarita had worked at the Spanish Embassy during our first five years, seen in Photo No. 42. Steve and his wife, Liz, had a baby boy called Marlin, who grew up in water, as a good marlin should! Steve was a professional caterer. After leaving The Driftwood Club, he opened his own restaurant in Malindi. It didn't do well, so he turned to outside catering in Nairobi. But he was an inveterate complainer. Seeing no future in Kenya, he finally decided to emigrate. His wife was a Kenyan citizen with a good job in tourism with Lonrho, and I believe she stayed in Kenya.

One family we got to know was the Griffiths. Tony and Wendy were Kenya citizens. He owned a secretarial college in town, and they lived in a house with a large garden in Miotoni Road in Karen. Their daughter was about the age of our girls. They also had a son called Craig, who later worked in the Masai Mara, before starting his own safari company. I recently met him in Lamu with his aging father.

Next door to the School Lane house lived Mr Davis, one of the founders of Davis & Shirtliff, with his son and family. The son has already retired as I write. Around the corner from the house lived a family with two girls at Imani School. We used to take it in turns with them and another family, to make the forty-five kilometre trip to Thika on Monday mornings and back on Friday afternoons. Stan Pick was Lebanese and his wife was English. The father of the other family was Kitili Mwendwa, the Attorney General. They were *Wakamba* from Kitui. One day, he had an accident in his Mercedes on the way to collect his children from school. He died that day. I often wondered if his death really was accidental. Fortunately, he was alone in the car at the time of the accident. His wife later went into politics and became the MP for her area.

The road to Thika was in a bad state of repair, but after some time, a new dual-carriageway was built. It seemed to take years! During its construction, there were many diversions, and the journey was long and frustrating. Unluckily for us, the girls were about to leave the school by the time the road was fully operational. Nowadays, a 'super highway', built by the Chinese, has transformed travel between Nairobi and Thika. For some time after it opened to traffic, there were no signs and no road markings. Imagine the chaos! Fortunately, these 'minor details' have been put right. At least we now know where we are going! Discipline still leaves much to be desired, however!

During the time I worked at the bakery, Nairobi was growing apace. It is a pity that the road network did not grow in tandem with the growth in population and motor traffic. More and more rural people were flocking into the City in search of work, and the estates and slums of the southern and eastern suburbs were spreading outwards, with no planning at all. More and more Kenyans wanted cars: for the growing middle class it was a status symbol. However, it was still possible to drive to work in the Industrial Area without too much trouble. These days, any journey within Nairobi by vehicle is likely to be a frustrating affair. The value of time lost in productivity, and fuel due to traffic delays, must run into millions of shillings a week, let alone the pollution of the air. Only recently has some effort been made to enhance road communications within the city, including a new Super-Highway, subject to a toll.

The fourteen-seater *matatus* ply the commuter routes in their thousands, supported by an inadequate bus fleet. There is no doubt that they provide an essential service, but the time has come for a huge investment in the infrastructure for the City. The *matatus* are badly maintained, driven without due regard for other road users and often overloaded. They also account for a disproportionate number of accidents. But they have power, because they know they have become indispensable. Recently, a new menace has come to haunt Nairobi roads; the motorcycle. They carry goods and passengers in their thousands, riding on pavements, through red lights and the wrong way along one-way streets. One has to be so careful while walking. Sadly, nothing whatsoever is done to curb their disgusting behaviour!

It was during our 1980 summer leave that we made an infrequent visit to Harwell to see Nanna Hawley. She and Grandad had moved from Green Harbour in 1961 or 1962, to stay with his daughter, Midge, due to his failing health. He passed away in January 1963, but Nanna was about ten years his junior, and went on to live until her mid-eighties. Photo No. 58 shows Isabel and Cathy with their 'Nanna Biscuits' on her eighty-third birthday, the 24th July 1980. Nanna was given that Biscuit label due to her normal practice of offering tea and biscuits to visitors.

Margarita was giving Spanish lessons in our School Lane house to an American who ran the Kodak business in Kenya. It was at the time that I began to think of a change of job, after nearly three years with Elliot's Bakeries. It was not considered advisable to change jobs too often: it gave the impression to a would-be employer that the person could not 'hold the job down.' On the other hand, staying too long in one position could lead to boredom, especially for an accountant, who prepares Accounts and budgets on a regular basis. An interviewer wants to see varied experience. I decided that three years was enough to show that I was on top of the work. Margarita must have mentioned my interest in getting a better job, and I have to thank her for that. The American gave me a valuable piece of advice, which may have helped me to secure a good senior management position in an international company. He said that a good curriculum vitae was essential; not too long, so that the reader doesn't become bored before reaching the end, but at the same time containing all the required information; family situation, educational qualifications, work experience, future plans and expectations, hobbies and interests, etc. The CV must capture the interest of the reader, so it should be professionally typed, well laid out and clear. The covering letter should be hand written and should 'sell' the writer. In my career, I have interviewed many job-seekers, and read hundreds of job applications. Most of them make the mistake of writing a stereotype letter, often pleading with the recipient to employ them. The employer wants to read that the person has something to offer, not to feel that they are trying to arouse the sympathy of the reader. After all, the employer is looking for someone who will add value to the business, not to give a job to someone out of pity.

The American advised me to write to the head offices of all the multinational companies with business in Kenya, rather than to the local offices. I secured the addresses and wrote about thirty letters. I received only a few replies and they were all negative, except one; The Coca Cola Company in Atlanta, USA. They wrote that there was a vacancy in the Nairobi office for a Regional Finance Manager, and I should contact a Mr. Ferrari, which I did. Mr. Ferrari called me for an interview. Well before the end of the interview, I saw that Mr. Ferrari was going to offer the job to me. He told me that he was required by the Immigration Department to advertise the post in Kenya, specifying the applicant should be a Kenya citizen. But he said that it was a mere formality: the job was already mine. So that is how I came to join Coca-Cola Africa Limited. I worked there for almost nine years, beginning in September 1981.

While still at Elliot's, I had interviewed and employed an assistant accountant. Out of all the letters of application, his was different, and at the interview he had come across as a bright, forceful and honest young man, and one who seemed as if he knew where he was going. John Mucai did not disappoint me. I had been with Coca-Cola for a year or so when I asked him if he was interested in following me. He did just that, and when I finally said goodbye to an office job in 1990, he succeeded me in the position of East Africa Region Finance Manager.

COCA-COLA AFRICA LTD

A NEW JOB MEANT A new house. The School Lane house belonged to Mercat. Estate Agents were not common like they are today. They did exist but Margarita had a novel way of bypassing the professionals, and she succeeded in finding a wonderful house. She chose preferred areas, and drove slowly around, looking for empty houses. When she saw one, she would ask a watchman or neighbouring gardener for the telephone number of the owner. In this way, she discovered a house in New Muthaiga that seemed not to be occupied. She took the telephone number, called a Mr. Mohindra and made an appointment to see him. The house had been rented by an Israeli security company, the bosses of which had suddenly upped and left, leaving behind them a lot of equipment, including a telephone switchboard and dozens of telephone handsets. The garage had been used as the control room, and in front of the house a wireless mast had been set in a strong foundation. The garden and the house itself needed some work to make it habitable. Mr. Mohindra was a businessman, and part of the family that owned the JVC franchise in Kenya. He must have seen that here was a person who would be a reliable tenant, who was willing to put in some work on the property. It must have impressed him too that we were Coca-Cola expatriates. Although the house was clearly worth more than Shs.12,000/- per month, (but a tidy sum in 1981), he agreed to that amount. The Company limit was Shs.10,000/-, but we decided that it was well worth it to pay the extra Shs.2,000/- ourselves.

The house was situated on Thigiri Ridge Road, a small unmade road off

Thigiri Ridge. It was set in seven acres of land, about one-and-a-half acres of which was developed garden, with several mature Flame trees in front. The house was white with a Scandinavian-style high pitched tile roof. There were five bedrooms upstairs, one of which we made into a television room, and two bathrooms. The ground floor had a large kitchen, dining and sitting room and an office. The sitting room French doors opened onto a patio, which led to a lawn and flower beds. It was a dream house for us at that time.

The day we moved into the house, we left everything in a mess and went to the wedding of Noor Adamali's brother. It was a Saturday and it rained. Noor owned a furniture making business called Woodcharm, with a showroom and workshop in Kijabe Street. He had made hardwood reproduction furniture for the Spanish Embassy, and he was now called in to make furniture for our new house. Coca-Cola had given me a very generous settling-in allowance, which covered quite a lot of furniture. He made a dining table and chairs, a sideboard, a corner cabinet and a desk. Those were the things I remember. The sideboard was inlaid and it was Charles Spackman who did the work. His big problem was beer: he loved his beer and could drink a dozen bottles in a sitting. But one day, he contracted black water fever, and his liver was unable to take the punishment. He succumbed to the disease. He was only in his forties, I think.

The two sofas were bought at Interior Designs and were of good quality. The next time we went to England, we bought enough of a beautiful, expensive material from John Lewis to cover the suite, and make full length curtains for the sitting and dining rooms. We managed to smuggle them through the customs in our suitcases, which was extremely naughty of us. That material lasted for years and years. Both suite and curtains accompanied us to our next home after New Muthaiga and looked almost new fifteen years into their lives. It is not worth buying cheap. In the end, it is the best quality that lasts, and turns out to be the best value for money. There was another acquisition that came through Kenya customs in the suitcase; a stereo system, admittedly not the biggest but nevertheless a bulky set, with amplifier, turntable and two speakers. One good thing about being an expatriate in

Kenya was that the customs men hardly ever bothered to open the luggage. At that time, if you happened to be a Kikuyu lady with three heavy suitcases, you would likely be importing clothes for sale, and the sharp-eyed officials would have their arms deep in the cases in no time. With *mitumba* clothes so cheap now, it is not really worth the bother, unless they are new clothes for up-market shops. These days, customs officers are on the lookout for drugs.

We brought Jackson Amuyunzu with us from School Lane. He had come to work with us when we lived in Mpaka Grove and had followed us to Davidson Road. He had somehow learnt that we had come back to Kenya in 1978 and had miraculously reappeared on the scene. We had taken him back, and in 1981, when New Muthaiga became our home, it also became his. But despite the improved conditions, he was unhappy with the move, and soon began a campaign to register his strong disapproval, in ways I will come back to. His complaint was that the new house was far from the local *duka,* (shop). To have to walk further for his maizemeal and other necessities was inconvenient, and he believed that his campaign would result in a move back to Westlands. He soon had his brother working for us as the *shamba* man, (gardener). Japheth was a young man from the village, big and strong, and under his brother's thumb. Thanks to this dominating attitude of Jackson's, we got through two house girls very quickly! He thought that it was right that he should be the one to rule the house. But with two young girls at home, we knew it was advisable to employ a woman. Jackson did not understand our ways, firstly the move from Westlands to faraway New Muthaiga and then employing a newcomer in the house, especially a woman.

Having a big house and extensive garden had its disadvantages, as we were to find out. The lawnmower was forever breaking down and had to be driven to the mechanic. The upkeep of big houses and gardens entails a lot of work, and that means staff, and more staff the more problems. Apart from the three workers already mentioned, Coca-Cola paid for a night *askari,* as well as an alarm system. Often, when returning from an evening out, we would hoot at the gate in vain for the man to open up, and one of us in the car would have do it for him. On one occasion, coming home late, when there was no moon to light the way, the walk across the grass in search of the missing man resulted in one of us tripping over his sleeping form. He vehemently denied being asleep. *'Mimi hapana lala!'* he uttered sleepily. With this level of professionalism from our security man, I had my fears, especially when the night wind brought creaks and bangs to the house, and at times when there was no electricity to power the security lights and the alarm. Our house was isolated, and the unkempt land sloped down to a small river at the bottom, providing plenty of cover for waiting, as well as departing, thieves. I will admit I spent some anxious times, if I happened to lie awake in the night.

It is well known that most house robberies are 'inside jobs', meaning one member of staff does a deal with an outsider to steal, the proceeds being shared. I believe we treated our staff well, and therefore we suffered less than many others. I will come back to the problems Jackson gave us later.

But there were pleasures in plenty in our New Muthaiga house. The red soil was fertile and I worked a vegetable garden, growing, with varying success, several kinds of crops. The most exciting were the *pimientos de Padron*. One year, during our annual visit to La Coruna, I brought back some seeds of this special little pepper that grows in a part of Galicia near Santiago de Compostela. They look like the very hot variety but they are mild but tasty. I managed to harvest a good crop in the rich red soil of New Muthaiga. We also had a big avocado tree behind the house. The avocadoes were big and creamy. In the season, they were enjoyed by the family, friends, the Olive Thrushes, the cats and the odd stray dog. Avocadoes are one of the only 'complete' foods, containing everything the body needs. A group of banana plants was also established next to the vegetable garden. To the side of the back garden there was an orchard of macadamia nut trees. They had long been neglected; the grass and weeds growing thick beneath the slender trunks. We did harvest a few of the round, hard nuts, but macadamia trees need a lot of attention to produce a good crop, something we never got around to giving them.

Our garden was home to many varieties of birds. Over five hundred species have been recorded in Nairobi. The acres of garden, hedges and bush, and the hundred metres of river bank provided a rich habitat. A short walk from the house was the entrance to Karura forest, parts of which were still endowed with indigenous trees. These were home to turacos, babblers, brownbuls and many forest birds, many of which I was unable to identify, sometimes only hearing an exciting call tantalisingly close; the form itself hidden in the undergrowth. In the garden, the white-browed robin chat was one of the common residents, nesting in the thick tangle of lantana and bougainvillea. The air of early morning rang with the plaintive sound of the divine duet. Loud and raucous was the call of the hadada ibis, as it flew overhead on its way to its daily feeding ground. Striped swallows regularly nested in the eaves of the roof. The black kite was a frequent sight; wheeling and swooping, its forked tail twisting to and fro. Eating a sandwich on the lawn was a risky affair. Black kites are capable of swooping in low and taking the sandwich from one's hand in the twinkling of an eye, often inflicting a wound on the hand in the process. I once saw a harrier hawk raiding a nest, hanging upside down, while it robbed the nest of young birds. In spring and autumn, the migrants would pass through; the yellow orioles with their liquid notes, the European swallows strung on the telegraph wires, the tiny warblers and many others. Throughout the year I saw a variety of doves, bee-eaters, woodpeckers, sunbirds, and a host of other interesting species. For colour and daintiness, it is hard to beat the sunbird family, of which there are about forty species in Kenya. Telling one from the other is often difficult. For me the scarlet-chested sunbird takes the prize, with its almost black plumage and brilliant scarlet breast.

While living in New Muthaiga, we safaried less, choosing instead to relax in the garden during the weekends. Many of our early English friends had by this time returned to the UK, but we continued to socialise with the Mexicans. Lunch parties in the shade of the trees were a common feature of Sundays. The official language of Kenya being English, all the staff of the Embassy spoke the language fluently, so that a mixture of Spanish and English would flow across the table, tongues loosened by good Spanish *rioja* and home cooking.

A word about Mexican food while we are on that subject. It is hard to believe that, if the New World had not been 'discovered,' many of the foods we take for granted would be unknown to us. Take for example, corn, or maize as it is better known. Today, it is the staple food of much of Africa, so much so that many Kenyans, for example, do not consider that they have eaten unless they have had their *ugali*. Yet maize was brought by the Portuguese, who had only recently brought it from America. Potatoes have become a staple in many countries, notably Ireland, where the potato famine caused mass starvation. Tomatoes, avocados, chilies and chocolate are all native to America. All the English words for these foods came from ancient American languages via Spanish. What would we do today without them? Mexican cooking relies heavily on these ingredients, especially maize, from which they make a surprising variety of dishes. The Europeans knew nothing of tobacco before Sir Walter Raleigh brought it to England in the 16th Century; at least that is the history we were taught at school. In Spanish schools, the children were taught that Raleigh and Drake, those knighted English 'heroes' were nothing but pirates!

Christmas 1981 saw the visit of my sister, Jean and her family. Jean and Richard had wedded in 1972, and now had two children, Paul and Claire. Two memorable safaris were enjoyed during their visit; one to El Karama Ranch, on the River Ewaso Ngiro in Laikipia, and the other to Lake Baringo. We had been to both those enticing destinations before, and knew that our visitors would love both. We stayed in a small lodge on the shore of Lake Baringo. Sadly, following some years of above average rainfall, the lodge is now under water; a situation shared with other lakes in the Rift Valley. Photo No. 59 shows the Alexander and Hawley families posing in front of the lake. Always a favourite venue for us, the River Ewaso Ngiro was a happy playground for bathing, or just sitting, listening to the captivating sound of flowing water. In Photo No. 60, Jean and Richard are doing just that! In another Photo, No. 61, the four children enjoy playing in the water.

We had stayed in Lake Baringo Lodge on an earlier occasion. The lodge was set on a promontory of a small island, with a spectacular view across the lake towards the eastern wall of the Rift Valley, beyond which lies the

Laikipia plateau. The climate is hot, but the camp was handsomely endowed with fever trees, and of course there was a little swimming pool. Next to the dining room was a stone-floored lounge with a thatched roof, looking out over the brown waters. A bird table attracted many species, hornbills being the most memorable. Lake Baringo attracts hundreds of different birds, and being one of the beads in a necklace of lakes, it serves as an attractive passageway for the migrants on their way to and from Southern Africa. The lodge had moored a pontoon some hundred metres from the shore of the island, and we would swim out to it and dive from it. Apart from hippos, the lake was home to crocodiles, but apparently, they have never attacked humans. In fact, we did swim once from the shore of the mainland, and we could actually see them some way off. True to what we had been assured, they never interfered with us.

One couple we became friends with at this time was Andy Slone and his partner. One evening, we had gone to the Donovan Maule theatre, and in the interval, we had met the tall, bearded, dark-haired, smiling young man and his petite, equally smiling young companion. They had recently arrived in Kenya, and in the small Spanish-speaking community, the girl had been confused with my wife, Margarita. We soon learnt why! Her name was also Margarita, and she was from Leon, a province not too far from La Coruna. But that was not the only similarity between the two couples. Andy was an English accountant. No wonder people got the two girls mixed up! We soon became good friends. We used to go on safari together, for they were keen campers and interested in bird watching. Photo No. 62 shows them on one of our safaris together. We also spent a holiday on the coast with them, (Photo No. 63).

It was through them that we began smoking marijuana, or *bhangi,* as it is known in Kenya. Marijuana is another word from Spanish America. Hemp and Cannabis are the English names for the plant, the leaves and flowers of which the drug is taken. In its dried state it is normally rolled into cigarettes, or chewed. In Arabian countries, hashish, the resinous extract from the flowers, is smoked in a hookah. We rolled our own 'joints', and either in the privacy of home, or in the freedom of the bush, we would share a 'toke' with the Sloans. Smiles would quickly become giggles, and the jokes that would not normally be in the least funny took on a new appeal under the influence of 'the weed'. Food became tastier, sweet things sweeter, drinks more effective, and sex? Well, a new experience! We began to buy our 'bundles' in the Nairobi market, and sometimes we would smoke the two of us alone. I even kept some seeds and planted them in the bush down towards the river, until I began to fear that it would be discovered, since growing the plant is a criminal offence. It is a remarkably easy plant to grow and an attractive one to look at, with its large leaves, something resembling a maple leaf. I read somewhere that if hemp were allowed to be grown without restriction, it would solve many of the world's problems. Hemp is one of the most versatile, valuable and easily grown crops on Earth.

I had begun smoking cigarettes at the age of nineteen. I had also experimented with small cigars and even a pipe, courtesy of my maternal Grandfather, who sent me his well-used pipes by post! And the Kenya Customs inspected them closely! But having suffered with chest trouble following the bout of pneumonia in 1956, and from the effects of the London smogs, I quit the habit around the time I got married in 1967. Then, in the early eighties, I began to disturb my lungs again with 'dope.' I believe it is less harmful than tobacco and non-habit forming. I say this with authority, because we had no trouble doing without if necessary, and when Margarita and Andy went to work in Indonesia, they easily gave it up. But we began to make flapjacks laced with 'grass'. The effect is much the same, but it only takes longer to manifest. One day, we made and enjoyed flapjacks at home and waited. The results were far more explosive than I could have imagined. I had had a chest infection, and Dr. Sheth had put me on a course of antibiotics. Why had I forgotten? We had been told not to mix bhang and allopathic medicines. I would not wish anyone to go through the experience. I felt as if I was dying; there is no other way of describing the sensation. It is hard to say how long it took for that hopeless feeling to give way to a glorious high that lasted the rest of the day. Margarita and Andy had been called during the height of the 'emergency', and Andy had just laughed. It's only 'the rushes', he had declared, saying that it would pass. They came during my 'happiness' and shared in it.

That incident reminds me of another time, when Margarita and I experimented with something new. We had gone out one evening to Nargis Kapuripan in River Road, for chicken tikka with some friends. The restaurant is well known for its pan; the concoction of various ingredients, chiefly beetle nut, wrapped in a leaf, which the Indians keep in the side of the mouth, and which stains it red. Tobacco is an optional ingredient. We asked the man to throw it all in and went off happily, with the wad safely tucked into the cheek. We had not even reached home, when the hearts started beating like drums. We were sitting up in bed at three in the morning, unable to put our head on the pillow. Never again will we allow the optional ingredient to be added, if we ever dare to take pan again, although that is highly unlikely!

One Sunday in August 1982, the peace of New Muthaiga was shattered by something we could not have anticipated. It was the day of the attempted coup d'état; the day that a group of disgruntled air-force officers, backed by highly placed politicians opposed to President Moi's regime, attempted to overthrow his four-year-old Government. It was badly planned, but the whole of Kenya held its breath for twenty-four hours. During that time, there was widespread unrest and looting in Nairobi. Kenyans were advised by the Government to stay at home. From New Muthaiga we could hear the sounds of gunfire that day. Margarita and Andy stayed the night, rather than risk the journey home. The Government-controlled radio station, VOK, remained in Government hands. The following morning, I decided to go to the office in Bruce House. Driving through Westlands, I felt the eerie silence of a commercial centre normally thronged with traffic and with people going about their work. The evidence of looting was clearly seen, with cartons, paper and other debris strewn everywhere. Many shop windows were shattered and glass lay about. On the way to town, many abandoned cars stood looking in a variety of directions, where their drivers had left them in a hurry. The shops of town had not been spared by the looters. The same scene of desolation met me wherever I went. A few Coca-Cola employees with cars had risked the trip into town.

We called the Managing Director, and it was agreed that the office would remain closed until the situation had returned to normal. But by then, it was clear that the coup had failed, and a swift return to normal life was imminent. It transpired that the plot involved relatively junior air-force officers, who became the scapegoats. They were swiftly tried and executed for treason. President Moi's suspicions fell on Home Affairs Minister, Charles Njonjo, an accusation strongly refuted by the seasoned Kikuyu politician. He had supported Moi's succession on the death of Kenyatta, but he was now sent into the wilderness. Another victim of Moi's revenge was Raila Odinga, son of the Luo freedom fighter, Jaramogi Oginga Odinga.

With the death of Kenyatta in 1978, the new President had released all political detainees, bringing a sigh of relief from a Nation that believed the oppression of the Kenyatta years had come to an end. Following the 1982 failed coup, Moi became paranoid, seeing dissent and treason lurking in all the dark corners. Many prominent politicians found themselves in detention. Newspaper editors were warned to avoid controversial topics on pain of detention. Ordinary people whispered on the streets, afraid that they may be overheard by Government spies. Throughout the rest of the 1980's, the basement of Nyayo House was used by the Special Branch, to interrogate political opponents of the regime, and there were many claims of torture. These claims later came before the courts, and successful claimants were awarded damages for physical and mental pain inflicted on them by the State. Kenneth Matiba is one powerful leader who was allegedly tortured, and who suffered a stroke as a result. His political career was cut short, like many others of the time.

It was shortly after the unsuccessful coup that the Sarit Centre was built in the middle of Westlands. The turmoil prompted the owners to review their plans for the shopping centre, the first of its kind in Nairobi. It had been designed with a fifth level and more extensive parking but, unsure of the future, the proprietors scaled down their ambitious plans. In the event, Kenya went on to enjoy a decade of peace and development, and the Sarit Centre became a prosperous and popular shopping centre. In the years that followed, many shopping malls were built in all parts of the city, and in the provincial towns. Chain stores like Uchumi, Nakumatt and Tusky's expanded rapidly, taking a greater and greater share of the retail market, and keeping pace with the fast-growing middle class. However, new supermarkets, namely Naivas, Quickmart and French-owned Carrefour are now the leaders, while Uchumi and Nakumatt have shut down, perhaps due to unsustainable growth. Hypermarkets with car parking facilities are attracting a wider clientele. In the 1970's, it was the European and Asian population, as well as a small affluent African class that could afford a car. It is not so now. How life has changed in the last fifty years!

Prosperity and growth of the economy, however, has hardly touched the urban poor, the marginalised masses that inhabit the crowded slums of Nairobi, such as Kibera, Mathare and Korogocho. In these bundles of tin shacks, with leaking roofs and mud floors, millions eke out an existence in any way they can. In the hot weather, the insides of the houses become ovens and, in the rains, the earth roadways are transformed into mud baths. If the rain is extra heavy, even sewers will overflow, bringing the risk of cholera and other waterborne deceases. The slums are home to thieves and other criminal elements. In times of ethnic unrest, they are the first places to erupt into violence. The slums are inadequately policed, encouraging the residents to take the law into their own hands; even lynching suspected robbers. The preferred method was to beat the suspect senseless, stuff him inside a car tyre if one is handy, a then dousing the victim with petrol and setting him alight. These perpetrations draw crowds and many join in, I suspect in the hope of dispelling life's frustrations, even if they have no idea what the victim has done.

Despite the goal set by UNEP, water shortages continue to place a burden on the residents of the slums, some of whom never see piped water and have to spend precious shillings on water in yellow, twenty litre containers. The water may not even be safe for drinking. I know that in the 1970's, water shortages were there, but Nairobi had a population of under a million, compared to close to five million now. And meanwhile, the few remaining pockets of forest are rapidly being raped for timber, or carved up by land-hungry rural people, desperate for a plot to grow their food. The water catchments are under serious threat, and attempts by well-meaning politicians to resettle squatters, who have cleared virgin forest, never seem to bear fruit. And beneath it all is the devil called corruption that ensures that the 'big' people behind the illegal activities never get taken to court to face the justice system.

Successive Governments claim to wage war on corruption, which everyone says they want eliminated from society. But if the truth were told, Governments are not willing to stamp it out, and ordinary people cannot do without it, because they often want something done that is in some way illegal or, if it is legal, they want it done in reasonable time, and they are willing to pay extra to be able to achieve it. Corruption cannot be eradicated unless the people are willing to suffer delays and hardships: only then can the Government of the day make progress, if it also has the will. It has been that way since we arrived in Kenya more than fifty years ago. But, on the bright side, since multi-party democracy and the end of the Moi era, Parliament has a far stronger voice, and scams and corrupt practices in high places are more likely to be exposed. Having said that, I have yet to see a 'big fish' named, tried and punished.

While corruption was rife in the business community, Coca-Cola Africa Limited, in common with all subsidiaries of the Company, followed a code of conduct that forbade any form of bribery, kickbacks or any other corrupt deals. Employees found contravening this rule would face dismissal. Of course, Coca-Cola had a Public Relations Director, who was a well-known figure in Kenyan society, and who could pull strings where necessary. Charles Mukora had been a senior official in the sports world. He knew just about everybody who was anybody, and was able to fix up meetings for the Managing Director with senior Government officials. This would not be classed as corruption, for no money or benefit in kind would be passed over, but perhaps a relative might be given a job somewhere. The dividing line between corruption and acceptable business practice is a very thin one!

'I am not unknown in Nairobi,' Eddie Ferrari was once heard to declare. And it was true. Coca-Cola was one of the best-known companies in Kenya and, without a shred of doubt, their product was, and still is, the number one brand, familiar even to the nomads of the northern deserts. Eddie had a fierce exterior, and was feared by many of his staff. But deep down he was not nearly as hard as he looked. If he were angry he showed it, and the office quaked, but he was often in a good humour. Despite his Italian name, he was Belgian. The Belgians have a reputation for lacking a sense of humour, and certainly his style was not like the English. But I was his choice for the job. He made me welcome and looked after me until his retirement around 1988. He was a manager of the old school, preferring to run the business 'by the seat of his pants', as the saying goes. He had had some accounting training and knew how to read accounts and budgets, but these things were less important to him than a 'feel' for a situation. About computers he knew nothing, but then neither did I, until my last years with the Company!

During his time, The Coca-Cola Company decided to insist that their overseas offices introduced computers. I laugh when I think of the first desk-top computer that was purchased by Head Office in Atlanta and delivered to us. At the time, it was exciting, but at the same time, daunting to our accounts department, which had never set eyes on one. The Tandy had, among other programmes, a spreadsheet, and I began to use it for simple schedules. I soon found, however, that its memory was tiny, and as my spreadsheet grew, I ran out of memory altogether. That Tandy turned out to be a toy, just for practicing. In a matter of months, it was replaced by a PC, and it was then that I became conversant with Microsoft Windows. As time went on, I used it for more and more complex spreadsheets, for the preparation of monthly accounts and for budgets. Management needed up-to-date information quicker and quicker, and it was not long before we had to send our monthly figures in coded format over the telephone line using a modem. These disciplines are now commonplace, but at that time it was new, and Kenya was well behind in communications technology. Towards the end of my stay with the Company, we were having to submit all our financial information in this way, to very tight deadlines. I was often in the office late at night during month end and budget submissions. Often, we were forced to input the data over and over again, due to balancing errors and interference on the line. The main means of communication with Head Office in Atlanta and Division Office in Windsor, UK, was by telex; email being unknown at that time. The telex operator was an elderly man called John Masai; well-educated and genial. He used to tell me that 'old is gold.'

The Company occupied part of the tenth floor, and the whole of the eleventh floor of Bruce House in Standard Street. Most departments enjoyed the eleventh, while the lowly Accounts and Traffic, (Purchasing/ clearing), used the tenth. My department had about six clerks, a secretary and a typist called Miss Biggs. I don't think Miss Biggs had another name. Everyone knew her as plain Miss Biggs. She was half European and half Indian. She was a little fat woman in her forties, I would guess. She sat all day at a manual typewriter and typed cheques and remittance advices, and kept herself to herself. When the Company invested in electric typewriters, she refused one, saying she could only type on a manual one. She also declined to accept other work, if she was ever asked to type something other than a cheque. So, she continued with her manual typewriter until the day she left.

The Traffic Manager was Aziz Mohamed, an Ismaili Muslim of my age. We became good friends. He was a fixture when I joined, and worked there long after I left. He finally retired with thirty-odd years' service.

The spiritual leader of the Ismailis is the Aga Khan, the hereditary head of the sect. He is extremely wealthy, but wherever the community lives, his organisation is active in community projects, as well as schools and hospitals, built in his name and run as business enterprises. The Ismaili community is a close one, helping their poor members. They are different from most Muslims, in that they encourage their womenfolk to work. Aziz's wife ran a food business in the Industrial Area, serving cheap lunches to workers in the area. The current holder of the title, Aga Khan IV, Prince Shah Karim Al Husseini, has ruled since 1957, on the death of his grandfather. His father, the late Ali Khan, had a reputation for being a playboy, but his son has managed to avoid the reputation of his father. I was amazed to read that there have only been four Aga Khans since the first held the title in 1817!

On one subject I disagreed with Aziz. He said one day that Mahatma Gandhi was a bad man, and that Mohammed Jinnah, the Muslim leader who campaigned for a separate Muslim state, and who became the ruler of Pakistan, was a great man. This belief is entirely at odds with the generally accepted idea of the Mahatma being the liberator of India, and the ultimate non-violent crusader for freedom of the Indian subcontinent. Gandhiji was horrified at the prospect of partition, insisting that Muslims and Hindus could live and work together, as they had done for hundreds of years. Jinnah fanned the flames of hatred in the minds of the Muslims against the Hindus, and I believe he was a chief cause of horrific loss of life in 1947, when the Hindus and Muslims, each living as minorities in the other's homelands, escaped to safety in India and the newly created Pakistan. I often wonder what would have happened if Gandhi's dream of unity had been realised. Would the people of those two religious faiths have continued to coexist with their differences?

Apart from controlling Coca-Cola's money, supervising the accounts department, preparing monthly returns and annual accounts and budgets, one of my other duties was to attend the regular monthly stocktaking at the Concentrate Plant in the Industrial Area, which produced the concentrate that is sold to the Coca-Cola bottling plants to very strict regulations. The secrecy surrounding the ingredients for Coca-Cola is legendary. In fact, Merchandise 7X is only one of the eight constituent parts of the famous drink that is secret. There is no secret about the others, among them, caramel colour, vanilla and caffeine. Merchandise 7X is a mixture of many natural flavourings and extracts. The closely guarded secret is stored in a bank vault, but even then, not in its entirety. Senior chemists only know the part of the mixture that they are responsible for. The entire recipe is known to perhaps two or three senior directors, and perhaps even they will not know the whole secret. That is the information I managed to gather during my time at Coca-Cola.

The history of the first cola drink is fascinating. A chemist in Atlanta first prepared the drink as a medicine in 1886. It contained the extract of the coca leaf, from which cocaine is derived, and that is how the famous beverage got its name. Later, it was decided to remove the extract, due to the use of the coca leaf as a narcotic. Perhaps it is still used! Governments have from time to time tried to force the Company to divulge the secret, but without success. When Coca-Cola wanted to resume its production in India, after a long period of prohibition, the Indian Government wanted to make handing over the secret a condition of entry into the market. I doubt it was achieved.

The most famous trade mark of all time was designed by the proprietor's accounts clerk. He could not have known that his creation would still be advertised throughout the world nearly one-hundred-and-forty years later! The distinctive bottle was only introduced in 1916. Coca-Cola was not carbonated until about this time, and *that* only happened by accident! It was the CEO of the Company, Maurice Woodruff, who in 1923 went international with Coca-Cola. Since then the Company has expanded into the most widely marketed product the world has ever known. There is not a corner of the world where it is not available, and there can hardly be a person on this Earth who has not heard of Coca-Cola. During the Second World War, Coca-Cola became a kind of Ambassador, and American troops in all the theatres of war had access to the drink that was synonymous with home.

While I was working with the Company, around the centenary year, it was decided to launch a 'New' Coca-Cola, with a different recipe. It was either the greatest blunder ever made by any business, or it was the greatest coup ever staged. The new drink was a complete flop. Everyone threw up their arms in horror, saying the drink was a poor substitute for the original recipe that had hardly changed in a hundred years. Immediately, the old recipe was brought back under the name 'Coca-Cola Classic'. It very quickly outsold the new version, and after a very short time, the new drink was withdrawn completely from the market. The 'Classic' was dropped and the old recipe was again sold as plain Coca-Cola. Sales did not suffer in the least by this, and it makes one wonder if the whole thing was an advertising gimmick. In Photo No. 64, Hon. Mwai Kibaki raises his glass of Coca-Cola with Mr and Mrs Ferrari and the Public Relations Director, Charles Mukora.

I have often reflected on the impact Coca-Cola has had on the World, in terms of health, habits and the environment, in negative and positive ways. Whether creating a wealthy multinational, and enriching the shareholders has a positive or a negative effect depends on one's position. Certainly, many millions have earned a living as a result, whether as employees, distributors, retailers, kiosk owners or indirectly through the manufacture of inputs into the business. Overall, has Coca-Cola and soft drinks in general benefited the World or not? I am inclined to think that it has not. Soft drinks have a lot of sugar, refined sugar that is actually harmful to the health. Coca-Cola contains caffeine, which is addictive. Children particularly are at risk from premature tooth decay. It is well known that a tooth immersed in Coca-Cola will disappear in time. Powerful advertising has convinced billions of people that it is 'cool' to drink Coca-Cola, and that it enhances the taste of a meal. It has therefore changed attitudes and diets for the worse. In Nairobi now, workers are more likely to eat white bread and drink a soda for lunch, whereas in the 1970's, it would be milky tea. The health of the people is threatened by this change of habit. The change from glass bottles and wooden crates to plastic, for both bottles and crates, is another negative aspect of the production of soft drinks. But I am thankful for one thing, in Kenya at least, and that is the continuation of 300 ml. glass bottles, although more of that size is sold in plastic now than in glass. How long will it be, I wonder, before Coca-Cola is no longer sold in glass? In business, a change is usually brought about for economic reasons, not for the sake of the environment.

There is a lot to tell about my nine years, (1981 to 1990), with Coca-Cola Africa Limited, but that period spanned the birth of our only son on 27th December 1983.

CHRISTOPHER JAMES ANDREW

ISABEL WAS ABOUT TO TURN fifteen and Cathy was three months short of her fourteenth birthday, when Christopher was born in Nairobi Hospital. I was forty-two and Margarita thirty-five. I had said that two daughters would suffice, because I was not prepared to be paying educational fees in my sixties. But Margarita and the Almighty had other ideas. She 'knew' the moment of conception, she 'knew' it was to be a boy, and she had already decided to name him after his father. There was no doubt whatsoever in her mind about those things, and in the end, the heavenly decision was accepted by me wholeheartedly. I have never regretted bringing a son into the world, and I was content to pay university fees well into my sixties, chiefly because we could well afford it. In fact, if another little bundle had come our way, I would have been the first to celebrate!

The night before Christopher was born, the four of us were sitting in our big double bed, watching a film about Winston Churchill entitled 'Young Winston'. The girls were on holiday, it being Boxing Day. It was an interesting film, but we were interrupted by a flow of water into the bed, a sign that the baby was on the way. We piled into the car and drove to the hospital, leaving Margarita there to await the birth. I asked the Sister on duty to telephone me as soon as the contractions became regular and frequent, so that we three could prepare ourselves, and reach the hospital in time for the birth. A call came before 7 am the next morning, and we hurried to the delivery room, only to reach there five minutes after Christopher had popped out. I was disappointed, having attended the births of the two girls, but happy at the same time that it was a little boy, as the mother had prophesied. Of course, the girls were over the moon to have a little brother. The arrival of Christopher did not occur without a down side. But it was in 1982 that Margarita had started to experience a depression that was destined to reappear and dog her life.

It was the policy in Coca-Cola at that time for expatriates to be allowed to use their annual leave air travel entitlement to go wherever they pleased, as long as the cost did not exceed the cost of the business class ticket to their home country. In December 1982, one year before Christopher was born, we had decided to cross the Atlantic and then, on the way home, to spend Christmas with Margarita's family in Madrid.

I remember the day we left Nairobi. It was early December and the rains were particularly heavy. Jaime and Hector were taking us to the airport for the night flight. The rain that evening was torrential. Margarita was already very depressed and hardly able to pack a suitcase. However, we left that evening, and eventually arrived in Miami, Florida. There we spent a night, before hiring a car and driving up the East Coast to Disney World, where we spent three exciting days. For Margarita it was a trying time, but for the girls it was an experience never to be forgotten. In fact, three days were hardly enough time to take in all there was to see. There were many attractions in The Magic Kingdom, some interesting, others exciting and some downright frightening, like the ride on the big dipper, which takes place in semi-darkness. We spent a day touring The Epcot Centre, with its technological marvels. I doubt they would be considered marvels now, with the astonishing advance of technology. Of course, the crowds were immense, and it was hard to find our car in the sea of metal boxes in the gigantic car park!

Having been brought up in England, where the towns have a certain intimacy; a cosiness born of hundreds of years of slow development, I did not take to American cities. Miami was my first, but I have since visited New York, Chicago and Atlanta. None of them has given me the feeling of homeliness, like the cities and towns of my native land, with the possible exception of New York. American cities are dominated by the highway and the motor car. Streets are wide and straight. There is no turning a bend and coming unexpectedly upon a market or an interesting building. British cities are not normally allowed to be spoilt by huge advertising boards, whereas in America giant billboards stare down at you from every skyline, and streets are cluttered with traffic signals, signs and neon lights. Miami is a big city, and for me the epitome of the worst of its kind. Two other things about Miami surprised me; firstly, the extent to which Spanish is spoken by the inhabitants, and secondly, the number of rich, retired people who live within sight of the sea. Perhaps if I were to visit San Francisco or the towns of New England, I may change my perception of American cities.

From Florida we flew to San Jose, the capital of Costa Rica, by way of Havana in Cuba. San Jose reminded me of Victoria, the capital of Seychelles, because of its lack of large, permanent buildings. It looked like an oversized village, its little ramshackle houses and shops piled here and there. Margarita had befriended a young Costa Rican environmentalist at a conference that he had attended in Nairobi, and for which she had worked as a translator. This is why we had chosen his country as the venue for a part of our holiday. He was the Director of a new National Park that was being created around an active volcano, and which included a tropical montane forest, where several species of endangered poisonous frogs lived, endemic only to Costa Rica. He took us up to the top of the volcano, the name of which I forget. The park was not yet open to visitors, but he permitted us to climb down with him into the caldera, and see close up the yellow, bubbling sulphur lake and whiff its pungent fumes. It was a rare treat for us. Even when the park opened, visitors would not be allowed to venture into the caldera, but would view the seething yellow lake from a gallery at the top. He also took us on a walking tour of the forest. Costa Rica is a very small country, but it is very active in environmental conservation, largely due to his enthusiasm, I suspect. We stayed the last night in Costa Rica in a very run-down lodge, and slept in a dismal cottage without any facilities. It was not the ideal location for a depressed person.

We had been to America on an earlier occasion, before any signs of depression had appeared. It had been in the summer of 1981, after I had resigned from Elliot's Bakeries and before joining Coca-Cola. We had been friends of the diplomatic Mexicans for some time, and they must have put dreams in our heads about getting to know their country. Margarita's father and stepmother were waiting for us in Madrid, and we handed Isabel and Cathy over to them. They were going back to La Coruna by train. But when we should have been exploring the Mexican capital, we were instead enjoying free accommodation in a luxury Madrid hotel, courtesy of Iberia Airlines. The flight had been overbooked, and forty irate Spaniards were left behind, together with two less irate Kenya residents, who had learnt the hard way how to be patient in times of adversity. Not so the Spaniards! They shouted and waved their arms in true Spanish style. But it made no difference: the flight could only take as many as the plane had seats. Madrid was enveloped in a baking heat, but we enjoyed our forced stay, admiring the work of many Spanish painters in *El Prado* and strolling around the streets of old Madrid in the relative cool of the summer evening. Our flight landed in Mexico City twenty-four hours later than planned. But we had made no hotel bookings and we had arranged no travel itinerary. It was to be an 'as it comes' holiday. And it turned out to be one of the favourite holidays of my life.

Mexico City stands on the ruins of Tenochtitlan, the Capital City of the Aztec Empire. When the Spanish *Conquistador,* Hernan Cortes landed on the eastern shore of what is now Mexico in 1519, Montezuma II ruled over a great civilisation. Like all Native Americans, both North and South, the Aztecs had crossed the land bridge from Eastern Siberia to Alaska before the last Ice Age ended, and before the level of the sea had risen to cut the link between the two continents. It is generally accepted that all pre-Columbian peoples of America are descended from the Mongolians. From them, other advanced civilisations developed in Central and South America, two of the best known being the Incas and the Mayans. Curiously, the North American 'Indians' did not build beautiful cities of stone like their Southern counterparts, although, contrary to the belief of the conquering Europeans, who considered them savages, they were highly spiritual people. The Hopi of

N.E. Arizona is a good example. Equally curious is the ease with which the term, 'Red Indian' was preserved in our language. It was the Italian, Christopher Columbus, or more correctly Cristobal Colon, who set out from Cadiz and crossed the Atlantic in 1492, expecting to land in the East Indies, but 'discovered' America instead. When he saw the first Natives, he called them 'Indians.' History has been rewritten to correct some of the misconceptions perpetuated for hundreds of years in our White cultural beliefs. One blatant lie is the one claiming that Columbus discovered America. People had been living there for many thousands of years before he was ever thought of, and it is well known that Vikings from Scandinavia had landed in North America hundreds of years before Columbus. Another lie concerns the relative cultural development of the Europeans of the 16th Century, compared to the people of America at that time. Europeans were dirty, unhealthy and carried many deadly diseases. They had only recently discovered that the Earth is round and travels around the Sun. Many of the peoples they conquered, on the other hand, understood the workings of the solar system, and built sophisticated monuments according to sacred geometrical principles. They also knew how to keep clean. Yet our history had us believe that Europeans were eliminating savages. This is particularly so in North America, and only recently is the record being put straight.

Cortes' victory over the Aztecs was completed in 1523, following the murder of Montezuma in 1520, and the destruction of Tenochtitlan in 1521. His success was largely due to the fact that the Aztecs believed that the White men on horseback were Divine visitors; the man and the horse being but one body. The horse was unknown in America at the time, and so the new arrivals were welcomed with reverence. In addition, the Spaniards carried deadly Smallpox, to which they themselves carried a degree of immunity. The Aztecs were forced to kiss the 'holy' cross, and in this way, the disease was spread. They died like flies. I later read a fascinating novel entitled 'Aztec,' which pictured Aztec life before, and at the time of the Spanish invasion. What a spectacle that great city would present to the modern-day tourist! Why are men so destructive? What was the point of destroying such a prize?

We spent about four days in Mexico City, the biggest concentration of human beings in the world at that time, around seventeen million of them! Margarita is seen walking in the square in front of the Cathedral in Photo. No. 65. We visited the Aztec ruins and the pyramids, we took a boat on the canal, and we listened spellbound to the *Mariachis* in the evenings. These bands of musicians, regaled in splendid Mexican costumes with gigantic *sombreros*, will play your request for a few *pesos*. They are enormously popular, with the locals as well as tourists. But the City is heavily polluted, and regular traffic jams choke the streets and highways. We sampled this congestion first-hand the day we hired a car and took to the open road. The car radio blared out Mexican songs; heart rending ballads, glorifying the revolutionaries that brought them freedom from Spanish rule. The political scene may now be different, but in the 1980's, control of the country was firmly in the hands of a fabulously rich political elite, which perpetuated the rule of one political party, to the exclusion of all others. The majority of Mexicans are poor but they are a peaceful and patient breed and it would take a lot to rouse them to the battlefield.

We headed north, stopping off at the ruins at Tula. We marvelled at *las momias de Guanajuato,* arranged in a small museum. The area has virtually no humidity, so that dead bodies do not decay in the normal way. The locals have discovered a way to make money, by displaying their dear departed for tourists to gawk at. The guide will point out what caused the death of this or that person. Outside the museum, one can even buy sweets fashioned in the shape of the mummies inside! We motored north on cheap, badly refined petrol, as far as Aguascalientes (Hot Water), on the edge of the desert, which covers the whole of Northern Mexico. Then we turned south-west, through now forgotten places, to the much romanticised Acapulco. Although it hardly lives up to its name, we did find interesting the stunts performed by young boys, who risked their lives by diving from a high cliff into a chasm no more than a few metres wide. From Acapulco, we turned north again, driving through beautiful scenery and picturesque towns, on the way back to Mexico City. We had been away about ten days, staying in a different town every night, eating traditional food in local restaurants and roadside cafes. Mexican food is highly original and exceptionally tasty. Typical is beans and rice, *Moros y Cristianos,* (Muslims and Christians), the equivalent of *maharagwe* and rice of Kenya. I took photographs of the attractive towns, streets and churches, from which I later painted water colour paintings. I loved every moment of the journey; the food, the people, who are so down to earth, humble and friendly; the music. In fact, everything was wonderful!

That had been in 1981. Now, after our 1982 holiday in Costa Rica, we found ourselves back in Madrid, at Jose's flat, where Margarita's father and her stepmother were waiting for us. When he saw Margarita's condition he was extremely concerned and sat with her for long periods. His own wife had died in 1961 of depression at the age of forty-eight, and he must have suspected that Margarita's condition was hereditary. He called for medical help, and she was put on anti-depressant drugs. It was an unhappy Christmas for us.

On our return to Nairobi, we sought out a psychiatrist. Dr. Fazal was an Ismaili Muslim, who later operated a clinic at the Aga Khan Hospital. Over the ensuing years, we consulted him often, and in 2007, when Margarita again went deep into depression, he treated her once more. Does one automatically dislike one's psychiatrist, or was Dr. Fazal a particularly annoying man? Margarita certainly developed a dislike for him! But give him his due, he did discover the nature of her problem after Christopher was born.

Early in 1983, Margarita had come out of depression and during the early stages of pregnancy she had gone to stay for a while with my parents at Watersmeet. All was well until after the birth. On coming home from the hospital, she brought out the basket that she had bought, and Baby Christopher was placed next to our double bed on her side. New Year passed and work resumed for me.

It often happens that hormonal changes trigger post-natal depression in the mother. It happened that way to Margarita. The events of the 10th January 1984 will forever be etched in my memory. It was mid-morning. I was working at my office desk. The telephone rang, and the switchboard operator said that my wife was on the line. I took the call, not knowing what I was to hear. It hit me like a bombshell. 'Come and take your baby. I have taken all the tablets in the house.' I was incredulous! When it sank in what she had done, I told her I was on my way. I called Marion Bennett, the Personnel Manager, and told her briefly the situation. She said she would call St. John's Ambulance and have an ambulance sent to the New Muthaiga house. I flew down ten flights of stairs at Bruce House and drove the company Peugeot 504 like a maniac, shaking and mumbling to myself all the while, hooting and cursing if a slow vehicle was in the way. After what seemed like ages, I reached home. Rushing up to the bedroom, I found Margarita sitting on the edge of the bed, red in the face from the futile attempts to strangle herself with the straps of her dress. I quizzed her about the tablets. She showed me the empty packets. I slapped her several times, when my efforts to wrest the straps from her hands failed. I was angry as well as consumed by worry.

Before long, the ambulance arrived, and we rushed to M.P. Shah Hospital in Parklands, the nearest good hospital to our house. Marion must have stayed in the house with the Baby. In the Casualty Department, the doctor wheeled her into the treatment room and pumped out her stomach before admitting her to the ICU. By this time, she was unconscious. After some time, I drove home to relieve Marion. At that time, we were friends of Anne and Jack Spence, and I must have called Anne for help. I also called our own GP, Dr. Sheth. He wanted to put Christopher into Gertrude's Garden Paediatric Hospital in Muthaiga, on account of his tender age. I was adamant. I was not going to let anyone take away my Son. I was quite capable of taking care of him, with the help of friends during working hours. Besides, he may well have contracted an infection in the hospital: it was common. Dr. Sheth also questioned my decision to choose M.P. Shah rather than Nairobi Hospital, which he said was much the better option. Besides, a few more minutes would have made no difference. So, after she was out of danger, he had her moved to Nairobi Hospital, where she stayed for ten days.

I settled into a routine of work and caring for my Son. Before starting work in the morning, I would take Christopher to Anne Spence's flat in Norfolk Towers, having changed and washed him. She had two teenage girls of her own, and she had also trained as a nurse. I knew the two-week-old Baby was in good hands. During the day, I would find time to visit the hospital. After work, I would collect him and take him home and look after him until the next morning. I don't remember whether his mother ever asked about him on my daily visits to her hospital room. If not, I am sure I talked about him. It is a painful experience to hear your wife telling you that she could find no love in her heart for her own newborn baby. It was painful for her too, not being able to feel the love for husband or child.

In times of trouble, you learn who your true friends are. The only other person who rallied round, with the exception of the Mexicans, was Jane Wanjiru. She also had a lot of experience with children and she was a good support while Margarita was in the hospital, but more so after her discharge. I vindicated my decision to keep Baby Christopher at home. When we took him for his first checkup, Dr. Forbes, the paediatrician, was pleased with his progress. I was even more pleased, as can be imagined!

It was normal in cases such as hers for a permanent watch to be kept as a precaution, in case she decided to harm herself. One of those assigned to the task was a Mkamba girl in her early twenties. We were to have a long relationship with Tracy. In the hours during which she sat by Margarita's bedside, they talked. Tracy was well educated and spoke good English. She told Margarita that the pay was terrible at the hospital: Shs.15/- per day was a pittance, even in those days. She asked if Margarita would employ her as an ayah to look after the baby. So, on discharge from the hospital, we took Tracy with us to New Muthaiga, and she moved into the servant's quarters next to Jackson's. His nose was firmly put out of joint by the arrival of a woman. Tracy quickly established herself as Christopher's ayah and she stayed with us for several years. When Isabel had her own daughters in the late 1990's, Tracy became their ayah. From time to time, she displayed some arrogance and sometimes fell afoul of the mistress of the house, but she loved Christopher and he loved her. With training she turned out to be a wonderful cook. She mastered Spanish cuisine and made delicious cakes and sweets, In Photo No. 66, Tracy is cooking in the New Muthaiga kitchen.

I cannot remember how long that depression lasted, and it was a trying time for all, but finally she got better. Dr. Fazal had decided that the cause was the inability of her body to balance the minerals, causing swings of mood. He put her on lithium carbonate, a drug that had been found to combat Bi-polar. She was to take it every day for the rest of her life, and to submit to regular tests to maintain the level of lithium in the blood. Perhaps her mother suffered from the same condition, and if so, and had lithium carbonate been available in her time, could she not have gone on to live a full life?

Meanwhile, Christopher was growing. He did not have the benefit of suckling at his mother's breast as an infant, due to the medication, but it seemed not to have done him any harm. He was a healthy boy.

Video film had by now replaced the super 8 movie film, a big technological advance. Future generations reading this will laugh heartily, and even now my statement will draw a smile, for the bulky, mechanical video film of the 1980's is fit for the National Science Museum! But we were glad of the chance to capture precious moments for posterity, especially as super 8 and video films can now be rerecorded digitally, condensing the footage into an infinitesimal space. In this way, descriptions of events, however poetic, are swept aside by the visual image, the talk, the smiles and laughs, forever available at the tap of a screen! I never owned a video camera but sometimes I borrowed one. Isabel's sixteenth birthday lunch was recorded thus. The patio outside the sitting room of the New Muthaiga house was the venue on that hot, sunny January day in 1985. Mum and Dad were staying at the time, (Photo No. 67). They would escape the English winter weather, either in New Zealand or in Kenya. At the lunch were Maria and Fredy Reif, some Mexican friends and our dear friend, Jane Wanjiru, looking slim and girlish. Christopher was just over one year old. He loved the chocolate birthday cake. We were talking about the development of his speech; a favourite topic of proud parents. I was saying, three times I think, because it appears no one heard me the first or the second time; 'he says bird', much to the amusement of the audience, not only those sitting round the long-ago lunch table, but those grouped round the screen watching the film!

At that time, Maria was in her forties and was married to Fredy Reif. They lived in a pretty cottage on the corner of Eldama Ravine Road in Westlands, where their marriage ceremony had been held. Maria was from Ponferrada, in the Asturias Region of Spain. She had been married before to a Spaniard and had two children by him; Javier and Olga. Fredy was an enigma, a sixty-odd-year-old Austrian, with a background shrouded in mystery. He had a wife and four children in South Africa. I think even Maria knew little about him. Margarita and I spent a lot of time in their company. But we often wondered if he had been a Nazi, (unkindly perhaps). He was roughly my father's age and was therefore a young man during the Second World War. He was very amiable in company, and good to Maria, but we got the feeling that he had a certain streak in him; one he did his best to hide. He was the sporty, adventurous type, always shooting off on scuba diving trips, or mountaineering, or parachuting. Perhaps he had been in the German SS! We shall never know the truth. He left Maria when she was a neighbour of ours at Norfolk Towers in the 1990's. He was uncomfortable with Maria's turn to spirituality. Shortly after this, she retired to an ashram in India, and I believe she will end her days there.

Christopher's first steps and his early attempts at singing nursery rhymes were also captured on video film. We had acquired a young Jack Russell terrier, a spirited little dog, who features in a clip of Tracy and a toddling Christopher. Manda was with us until, one day, he just disappeared from the garden, and was never heard of again. Margarita had previously, during one of her better moods, taken over a Cocker Spaniel from a friend, who had decided that she couldn't keep the dog. As I recall, it had been reared in Switzerland, a more suitable habitat than a big garden in tropical Africa. It was not the ideal breed, as we were to find out. McDuff, or plain Duff, was forever in trouble with its long, golden hair. Its favourite resting place was the settee, especially during wet weather when the garden was muddy! The John Lewis upholstery suffered, and eventually Duff had to go back home.

Two other notable events, apart from the round of lunch parties at the New Muthaiga house, was an extravagant party Margarita organised for my forty-first birthday in 1982, (Photo No. 68), and the wedding party for our good friends, Margarita and Andy, who were married in a civil ceremony in February 1983. My birthday party was a closely guarded secret. I was diverted by the Mexicans from arriving home too early, and I was suspicious that something was afoot. But I could not have anticipated the size of the gathering. Margarita was at that time in very good mood, in one of those phases where everything and anything is possible. It was a veritable extravaganza, with hired musicians and all! The wedding party was a more sober affair, there being no relatives of the couple within Kenya. Later, in March 2008, I had an e-mail from Margarita in Spain, saying that she and Andy had celebrated their twenty-fifth wedding anniversary with a trip to Uganda, Kenya having disqualified itself because of widespread violence following the disputed 2007 presidential elections.

The exact year escapes me, but during one of Margarita's 'high' periods, a large gathering of Spanish-speakers was invited to a lunch party, accommodated in the field adjacent to the house, with a marquee in case of rain and as a respite from the hot African sun. The lunch was in honour of Wangari Mathai, the indomitable environmentalist, who later became the first African woman to win the Nobel Prize. She spoke to the gathering about the environment, (Photo No. 69). It was about that time that we played host to a prominent Luo politician, Peter Oloo Aringo, who was the Minister for Environment, putting to him our fears for Kenya's forests. Like many straight and honest leaders, he was later sacked by President Moi, no reason being given. Aringo heard the news for the first time on the radio. He had not been told in advance!

One result of the coming of Christopher in December 1983 and Margarita's illness was the disruption to my water colour painting spree. It must have been in 1980 that I had decided Mrs. Betts could not really help me anymore, and I would have to just practice and develop my style. From then until 1983, I had done a lot of work, while my own individual style had evolved and I had held a successful exhibition. That prolific three-year period suddenly came to an end, and it was to be ten years before I was to get into the swing of painting again. As my artistic inspiration left me, so I developed a love of reading poetry and learning it by heart too. I remember clearly those Monday mornings, when it was my duty to take Isabel and Cathy to Imani School, driving back to the office from Thika alone with my poetry book on the passenger seat. I lived a charmed life, for I know my attention was often on the lines of poetry, rather than on the road ahead. I used to walk around the garden in New Muthaiga, learning epic poems by heart. I learnt 'The Ancient Mariner' by S. T. Coleridge, 'The Ballad of Reading Gaol' by Oscar Wilde, 'Gray's Elegy', 'The Thorn' by William Wordsworth, and many shorter poems. Apart from sustaining my memory, I got immense joy from reciting these favourites of mine from memory, while walking alone, driving or just sitting. In the years ahead, my love for reading English poetry increased. 'The Elegy written in a Country Churchyard' by Thomas Gray remains my favourite poem, closely followed by Alfred Lord Tennison's 'The Lady of Shallot' and Wordsworth's 'Intimations of Immortality from Recollections of Early Childhood'. Another of my favourites is 'Fern Hill' by Dylan Thomas. I love the Elegy for its pure poetic beauty and Gray's ability to paint a picture with the minimum of words. The first lines are famous.

The curfew tolls the knell of parting day,
The lowing herd wind slowly o'er the lea,
The ploughman homeward plods his weary way
And leaves the world to darkness and to me.
Now fades the glimmering landscape on the sight
And all the air a solemn stillness holds,
Save where the beetle wheels his droning flight
And drowsy tinklings lull the distant folds,
Save that from yonder ivy-mantled tower
The moping owl doth to the moon complain

Of such as, wandering near her secret bower,
Molest her ancient solitary reign.
Beneath those rugged elms, that yew-tree's shade,
Where heaves the turf in many a mouldering heap,
Each in his narrow cell for ever laid,
The forefathers of the hamlet sleep.

Another part I love,

Full many a gem of purest ray serene,
The dark unfathomed caves of ocean bear,
Full many a flower is born to blush unseen
And waste its sweetness on the desert air.

And another,

For them no more the blazing hearth shall burn,
Or busy housewife ply her evening care,
No children run to lisp their sire's return,
Or climb his knees the envied kiss to share.

And again,

Let not ambition mock their useful toil,
Their homely joys and destiny obscure;
Nor Grandeur hear, with a disdainful smile,
The short and simple annals of the poor.

The boast of heraldry, the pomp of power,
And all that beauty, all that wealth e'er gave,
Awaits alike the inevitable hour,
The paths of glory lead but to the grave.

Can storied urn or animated bust
Back to its mansion call the fleeting breath?
Can honour's voice provoke the silent dust,
Or flattery soothe the dull cold ear of death?

And yet again,

Far from the madding crowd's ignoble strife
Their sober wishes never learned to stray;
Along the cool sequestered vale of life
They kept the noiseless tenor of their way.

But even these bones from insult to protect
Some frail memorial still erected nigh,
With uncouth rhymes and shapeless sculpture decked,
Implores the passing tribute of a sigh.

Wonderful imagery!

Wordsworth was an enlightened poet. Read his words from The Ode.

Our birth is but a sleep and a forgetting:
The soul that rises with us, our life's Star,
Hath had elsewhere its setting,
And cometh from afar:
Not in entire forgetfulness,
And not in utter nakedness,
But trailing clouds of glory do we come
From God, who is our home:
Heaven lies about us in our infancy!

Shades of the prison-house begin to close
Upon the growing Boy,
But He beholds the light, and whence it flows,
He sees it in his joy;
The Youth, who daily farther from the east
Must travel, still is Nature's Priest,
And by the vision splendid
Is on the way attended;
At length the Man perceives it die away,
And fade into the light of common day.

And,

Mighty prophet! Seer blest!
On whom these truths do rest,
Which we are toiling all our lives to find,
In darkness lost, the darkness of the grave;
Thou, over whom thy immortality
Broods like the Day, a master o'er a slave,
A presence which is not to be put by;
Thou little Child, yet glorious in the might
Of heaven-born freedom on thy being's height,
Why with such earnest pains dost thou provoke
The years to bring the inevitable yoke,
Thus blindly with thy blessedness at strife?
Full soon thy Soul shall have her earthly freight,
And custom lie upon thee with a weight,
Heavy as frost, and deep almost as life.

In later years, I found great entertainment in more modern poets, one of my favourites being John Betjeman, His poem I love most is 'The Subaltern's Love Song'. There are many other poems I love. I have recently learnt three wonderful poems written by William Butler Yeats and two by George Crabbe. I never quite understood the poetry of T. S. Elliot, although he is considered one of the greatest Twentieth Century English poets. My love of poetry led to a desire to create my own, and I did so later on, from 2005 until 2008. This poetic period led to a short-story-writing phase for two years, and finally to novels. This meant that my love for wielding a paint brush had been put into mothballs. But in 2021 I put away the mothballs and lifted the brush again for almost two years. In 2022 I took up poetry writing again, laying down the brush once again. This seems to be a pattern in my life.

I believe one should do things for the joy of the experience and not to seek or expect approbation from outside. Art is the expression of what one has inside and cannot be forced in any way. Producing art to order or for money is not art, in my humble view.

During the 1980's, Christopher was growing into a healthy and handsome little boy. Two charming photos of him illustrate this, (Photos Nos. 70, taken on the patio, and 71, with me). In due course, he was enrolled in Kabete Kindergarten, a wonderful little school in Lower Kabete Road, run by a European couple, Mr and Mrs Wood. Mrs Wood gave her children a good start in life. The school was strong on sports and drama, the latter activity instilling in our small boy a love of the stage. We have video film of his annual dramatic exploits at the end of the Christmas term. At three years old, he made a splendid lion, complete with roar and claw. Another year, he took part in Peter Pan. No children were ever left out: the whole school participated, and an enormous crowd of parents was always there to cheer on their little darlings. Christopher was never a competitive boy; content to be himself. I believe children become over competitive because of parental expectations. There were two boys in Christopher's class, Kendall Evans and another whose name we all forget. They were both from families that pushed their children to excel. At one sports day, the other was in tears on the podium because he was second to Kendall and not first. Photo No. 72 shows Christopher performing. He developed well and was happy at Kabete. In Photo No. 73, Christopher sits in the front row of his class.

Eventually, he moved into preparatory school in the second year, we having agreed with Mrs Wood that an extra year in kindergarten would be better for him. We chose a nearby school; Peponi House Preparatory School in Farasi Lane. He studied there for two years. As time went on, we began to get negative reports from the teachers, saying Christopher played about in class and was not attentive. We did not believe it was entirely his fault. So, we decided to move him to Kenton College, which at that time had made itself a good reputation. We never regretted the decision. From the moment Christopher started there he began to blossom. The existing Headmaster left soon afterwards, and Roger Hartley took over. He was there to say goodbye to Christopher at the end of Class 8 in 1996. I will never forget the Friday assemblies in the school hall. Mr. Hartley was a good man and a great encouragement to the children. I never came out of the assembly without a wonderful feeling of love.

The mid 1980's saw Isabel and Cathy graduate from Imani School after their 'O' Level examinations, Isabel in 1985 and Cathy the following year. Thanks to the generous support of Coca-Cola towards educational expenses, we were able to send the girls to a good private secondary school for 'A' Levels, where they would benefit from stronger competition than they would have had in Kenya. Both had done extremely well, passing in twelve subjects each. Mum and Dad were living at Watersmeet by then. We chose a school close by, so that the girls would be able to spend their short breaks with their grandparents. Queen Anne's School in Caversham, across the Thames from Reading, was only about seven miles from Theale. But Kenya was in their blood and they missed home. Cathy told me recently that those were two years she would prefer to forget. The Headmistress, Miss Audrey Scott, was an elderly lady, who had been Headmistress of Limuru Girls High School in Kenya. The story goes that she finally went mad, and ended her days in a mental home. Was it true, or just a malicious tale spread by disgruntled schoolgirls?

Isabel elected not to go to university, although she had a place at Surrey to do Food Science. Instead, she went to study French in Paris. She has always been good at languages and has mastered Spanish, French and Italian, and becoming reasonably adept at Kiswahili. I went to visit her on one of my business trips. She had an attic flat in the centre of Paris. What I remember most about the few days we had together is the hours we spent marvelling at the many masterpieces to be found in the *Musee Quay Dorsey*. We particularly admired the impressionists. Both Isabel and I have a special love for them.

Coca-Cola's leave travel policy allowed us to experience places for no greater cost than a leave spent in UK. But with my parents looking forward to our visits to England, and Margarita's aging father depending on seeing his only daughter every year, we were bound to include these trips in our annual leave plans. And how different were the two destinations!

No. 48

No. 49

No. 50

No. 51

No. 52

No. 53

No. 54

No. 55

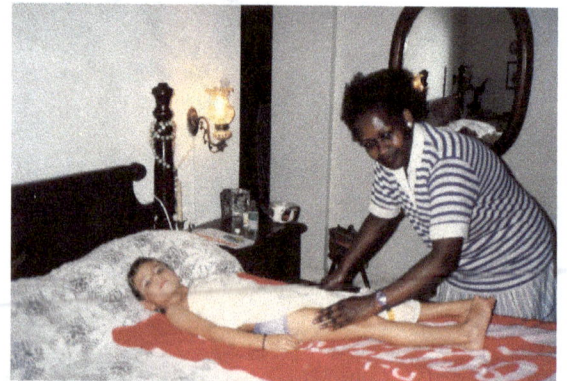

No. 56

No. 57

No. 58

No. 59

No. 60

No. 61

No. 62

No. 63

No. 64

No. 65

No. 66

No. 67

No. 68

No. 69

No. 70

No. 71

No. 72

No. 73

More recently, my sister, Jean sent me by e-mail a photograph of Watersmeet taken in the year 2008, showing extensive alterations carried out by the family that purchased the house from my parents in 1993. I instantly recognised it and it was hard to see what they had done; they had taken so much care to preserve the charm and character of the house. It is doubtful that Mum and Dad would have thought so. Mum told me she was not interested in going back there to see the house She had heard that the new people were going to extend it. When one has lived and loved a house as much as my parents did, whatever those who follow you do to change 'one's own home', it can only be a change for the worse. I think the house must have been constructed in late Victorian times, or perhaps later, in the Victorian style, built in red brick and with a gabled and tiled roof.

My parents moved from Upper Basildon to Watersmeet in Theale around 1979. Yew Cottage, with its large, developed garden, had been a dream house, after years in the Arabian Desert. They had toiled in the garden to produce organic vegetables, kept ducks, chicken and goats, reared litters of Golden Retrievers, and played host to paying guests. But there comes a time in life when one has to slow down, and scale down one's activities to suit the aging body. My father was at that time over sixty years old. Watersmeet was a perfect choice and a dream location for them. Bound by the River Kennet on one side of the garden and the Kennet and Avon Canal on the other, the sound and the smell of water was never far away, Photo No. 74 was taken from across the canal. Photo No. 75 shows my happy parents in the Watersmeet garden, with their Golden Retriever. Watersmeet was also more manageable. The lawns and flower beds still needed attention, but the vegetable plot was small and at the same time fertile. It was one of my mother's complaints when she moved into her final home in Blunsdon, shortly before Dad's passing, that there was no vegetable plot. But by that time, she no longer had the strength to till the ground, but with her determination, it was hard for her to accept that one comes to a stage in one's life when something that one has loved doing can no longer be done.

Our summer visits to Watersmeet in the 1980's would always include the inevitable early morning swim in the nearby lake; a reclaimed gravel pit. It would not matter about the weather. Come hail or storm, the dip in the lake was a family ritual from May until September. The 18th May, Mum's birthday, was traditionally the start of the swimming season. Any visitor to Watersmeet was included in the ceremony. There was always the choice, (and I may have opted out sometimes), but the pressure to comply was strong enough to entice the visitor to join the trek across the fields to the water's edge, if no further than that! In Photo No. 76, taken in 1990, we see the joy and enthusiasm of the family, trekking back across the field, no doubt looking forward to breakfast. Of course, the dogs would always be the keenest participants and the first in the water, stirring up the mud in the process. There were always two dogs in the family. As soon as possible after the older one had passed away; a puppy would be added. If it were not a member of the latest litter raised at home, it was a descendant of an earlier brood. Mum particularly loved her dogs, and even in her early eighties, when only Heather remained, she sometimes had the urge to have another. It is as well she did not.

Apart from walks along the canal, a lunchtime beer at a local pub, or occasional trips to visit relatives, we would enjoy the garden, particularly if the weather was hot. Fishing in the River Kennet, or submersing the body in cold but clear river water, would be favourite activities. The river was shallow but fast flowing, with a stony bed; hardly deep enough to swim. Photo No. 77 was taken outside the Bell Inn at Aldworth on one of our walks.

When it came to food, Mum was a traditionalist. Soup and salad were always the lunchtime fare, with homemade wholemeal bread and perhaps a glass of homemade beer to wash it down. Dad, sarcastically but good humouredly, referred to the soup as 'original', because he could never remember a day when homemade soup, often leak, was not served up at one o'clock. The evening meal was normally meat, potatoes and vegetables, and Mum would have to apologise if the last two were not from the garden. The meal was never complete without a sweet. I can see my father, sitting at the round, candle-lit table in the dining room, with the family around, tucking into a large helping of apple pie or apple crumble, with a generous helping of cream on top. My father never stinted himself when it came to eating! He loved his food and, because he led an active life, he never felt bad about eating well. He would brush aside all comments directed at his bulging body and, puffing out his chest, he would deny the existence of any fat whatever, claiming it to be pure muscle. To be fair to him, you could not say he was fat. Round he was, but fat he was not! Mum was not far behind when it came to appetite. And there was never a moment in the day when she was not engaged in some task or other. And she kept Dad on his toes too. The after-lunch forty winks were fine but the forty-first wink was disallowed. 'Charles, you were going to do so-and-so', or 'Charles the so-and-so needs doing', would drag him out of a comfortable sleep in the chair. If he dared to turn on the television during the day, within a short time his wife would come into the room, make a pointed remark and turn off the switch. It was not often that he would react. He would usually complain under his breath, and go and do whatever 'so-and-so' needed doing. The 'Walker' spirit was dominant. I think that if my father had married a docile or a lazy woman, he would have achieved much less in his life, like his father and his younger brother, Eric, whom I have described earlier.

Our 1984 summer leave in England featured Christopher's Christening in July in Theale Parish Church, the venue of my own in the war years. Jaime Cordero, as a Godfather, and his partner, Hector, came over. Photo No. 78 shows, apart from our own family, a good number of Kenya friends; Carole and Tony Fletcher, Lynn and Andy Barrett, Anne and Phil Dobson, Jane and Andrew Little, as well as Godmother, Tere Dolan and family. Margarita's nieces, Margarita and Natalia, represented the Spanish side of the family. Another photo taken during that time shows our family in Watersmeet garden, (Photo No. 79).

Nanna Walker celebrated her ninetieth birthday in great style at Uncle John and Auntie Dorothy's house in Rickmansworth in September 1985, and we were there to celebrate with her. Her two sons, Alan and Michael, were conspicuous by their absence, but the five daughters were there, together with their husbands, children and grandchildren. What a party! And what a huge issue! (Photo No. 80). It was a proud day for Nanna, who, at ninety and suffering from arthritis, surprised us by knocking out some old tunes on the piano in the evening. It was to be her last great get-together with her family. She passed away in 1987 at the age of ninety-one.

In late Autumn of that same year, 1987, for some reason I spent a holiday in England without the family. I remember going down to Torquay in Devon to stay with old Kenya friends, Roger and Pricilla Porteous. But what I remember most about the holiday was the hike I did with Mum and Dad across the Berkshire Downs as far as Devizes. Dad, the stick-in-the-mud that he was, was not so keen on the idea of walking miles without a laid down route and a timetable. But that is where he differed from Mum and me. For us, it was an adventure to set off, carrying only the minimum on our backs, the cool breeze in our faces and the springy grass under our feet, and just see where we ended up. We began the hike from Richard's pub in Baydon, on the edge of the Downs. Jean recalls that at that time she and her new partner, Henry were living in Swindon. It was the time that Richard's dog, Catkin, ran off while being taken for a walk and was never seen again. We three hikers took the ancient Ridgeway path, descending into Wanborough in the late afternoon, exhausted and hungry. That night, we stayed in a small inn, ate greedily, soaked our tired feet in warm water and laughed at everything, especially Dad's complaints about the hardship involved. A full day's walking on the Ridgeway brought us on the second night to Avebury, the site of the famous prehistoric stone circle. We stayed in Avebury and, on the last day, we followed the canal to Devizes, where we put in a rescue call to Richard, for him to come to pick us up in the car. It was a memorable walk, those three days of trudging the tracks. How quickly motorised transport brought us back to Baydon!

The Spanish part of the holiday was always a great contrast to the English one. Instead of English country walks, there were swims in the refreshing waters of the Atlantic Ocean, which pound the rocks and lap the *rias* of Galicia. On Sundays, invigorated by sea salt and hot sun and with the minimum of clothing, we would pile into one of those typical seaside restaurants, together with dozens of other families, all with the same intention; that of enjoying the weekly treat. Mother especially would perhaps appreciate not having to cook, or supervise the cooking. Crusty bread and a bottle of wine would soon adorn the table. Margarita's father would immediately attack the bread, selecting the crust and discarding the soft inside. Bread and wine would be well depleted by the time the seafood, *sopa* or *ensalada* was brought. In fact, should the owners know Don Pio, they would also know not to delay the food. He has been known to walk out of the restaurant, having become tired of waiting and having devoured the bread and drunk at least a glass of wine! A succulent dish of meat and potatoes would follow the fish course and, to fill the remaining space in the stomach, the *postre* came next. In the summer, the menu would not be complete without *melon,* otherwise *tarta* or ice cream. Coffee and, for the stout hearted, a brandy and a cigar were readily available. The Spanish love their food and, in my experience, one can hardly eat better anywhere in the world for a very reasonable price, in the informal restaurant atmosphere.

Don Pio never swam. In fact, he was hardly ever known to take off his shoes and socks on the beach; perhaps his jacket if it was particularly hot. He never carried money with him. Payment of the lunch bill was the duty of his wife, or a competitor for the privilege. I soon came to know the custom of paying the bill. A great show is made at the time of payment. I was often accused by Margarita of showing myself to be mean, because I was often shy at digging in my pocket. All sorts of tricks are perpetrated to secure the honour of being the first to pay, either by cornering the waiter early in the meal and telling him to be sure to bring the bill your way, or going to the kitchen to pay, as soon as the last course has been served. I found it rather embarrassing and actually hated the theatricals. One such Sunday lunch, I was tipped off that Lolita had gone to the kitchen to pay, and so, not wanting to appear miserly, I went in search of her. There ensued a bout of wrestling in the kitchen between us. I forget who won the privilege of paying; it really doesn't matter, but at least I did my duty.

Margarita's father had a twin brother, Joaquin. Their mother had died at the time of giving birth, and the twins were separated. Pio had gone to live with his paternal grandmother in La Puebla del Caraminal, a seaside village to the south of Santiago de Compostela. Joaquin had been brought up by an Aunt, who had a big old house in Muxia, another fishing village to the west of La Coruna, close to Finisterre, the westernmost point of the Iberian Peninsula. The Aunt's parents had made money and were among the first to own a car. They paid for the construction of a road from the nearest main road to Muxia, several kilometres long, so that they could reach their house in comfort. The house in Muxia was used during weekends and holidays by *Tio* Joaquin and family. Muxia became a favourite place for us. Joaquin was a celebrity in a village of fishermen, and being a surgeon, he often helped out with medical cases in the village. The house faced the main square and the sitting room window looked out onto the sea. Many a wonderful morning was spent in the sea, on the beach, or sunning ourselves on the rocks. We sometimes walked out of the village, past little fields enclosed by low stone walls, and into a sandy bay to swim, or walk up the rocky coast to a tiny church on a promontory, where the furious sea lashes the rocks in wild weather, and many a ship has floundered in heavy seas. The church was a place of pilgrimage for the local residents of the area, who once a year would suffer the kilometre-long ordeal on hands and knees as a penance. I remember one typical late Spanish lunch in that house, after a morning on the beach. It may have been in the 1970's. Don Pio's elder sister, Natalia was visiting from Argentina. At that time, she was a little round woman in her seventies, voluble like her brother, Joaquin, the outdoor, sporty man. In contrast, Pio was more serious and studious, but not without a sense of humour.

Joaquin's wife, Dolores, or Lola as she was known, was a hearty woman and very house-proud. The Muxia house was no palace, but she was very particular about her things: 'beds are for lying on, not for sitting on'! Turning on the tap in the kitchen, after she had cleaned the sink, would draw criticism. After her son, Quiquin left home to get married, the pride in her flat in La Coruna became a mania with her. After the death of her husband, she had nothing much to do but clean her flat, and we heard that she even discouraged visitors, in case they should disturb the tidiness of her home. We ourselves bore the brunt of this mania in the Muxia house. She allowed us to stay there on our own once. A pipe burst and flooded the house, not by any fault of ours, but the fuss she made and the accusations that flew around, made us not want to go back there without her presence. But I have fond memories of Muxia. However, one negative occurrence comes to mind: I left my camera on the beach. Only later, when in the house, did I realise. Going back, I found the camera washed by the sea water and totally ruined! At one time, we thought of buying a house in Muxia. In the end we settled for a house in the south of Spain, but that was in the early 1990's.

Our connection with Andalucia began with a holiday we spent there, when Christopher was 18 months old. It was July 1985. Isabel was sixteen and about to start her boarding school life in England. Cathy still had one more year at Imani School. A Danish Imani School parent had invested in a condominium in *El Cortijo Grande,* a development in the dry Province of Almeria, and had offered us a chance to stay there. Although the condos were nothing to get excited about and the finishing and furnishing decidedly dull, the setting was spectacular. The unit we had overlooked the golf course, bone-dry yellow at that time of the year, but with wide views of surrounding hills. Facilities included a swimming pool, bar and restaurant. We explored the area, which was popular with foreign investors, as was much of the Mediterranean coast of Spain. The small town of Mujacar in Almeria is a first-class example of how foreigners have infiltrated the pretty white towns of Andalucia. In the case of Mujacar, foreigners, and particularly the British, have established themselves as a major presence there.

The following year, 1986, we booked a flat in a new development near Estepona and ten minutes' walk from the sea. The brochure proudly advertised facilities such as a restaurant and shopping precinct. The flat we took was billed as the property of Ballesteros, the famous Spanish golfer. The two weeks stay cost over US$2,000. Imagine the disappointment we felt on arrival, to find it incomplete. There was no restaurant, no shopping precinct, and the block in which the 'Ballesteros' flat was situated was the only one finished. The rest was one big building site. One can see the state of it in Photo No. 81. Just as well, there was a good swimming pool. However, we put our disappointment behind us, as well as our skepticism about the famous 'owner' of the flat, and went on to enjoy our holiday. We travelled up the coast by bus, visiting Puerto Banus, Marbella and down to Gibraltar. Maria and Fredy Reif were staying not far from Gibraltar, and we went to see them. We also took a tour up into the mountains, to the picturesque town of Ronda. The charm of it was to haunt us in the years to come, and it was there that, in 1992, Margarita and I started our hunt for a Spanish dream house.

For us, the holiday was not marred by the dishonesty of those responsible for selling the package. On the other hand, we did feel for those foreigners who had retired, sunk their life savings in a retirement home in the sun, and moved there to such developments. We laughed at the arguments that went on daily between an Englishman and a German over a day-bed by the pool. The Second World War was being fought all over again! Each day, there was a competition between the two protagonists to see who could stretch his towel over the bed first, in order to book it for the day. There was more than one bed, and plenty of room around the pool. What was the attraction of that particular bed and that particular position? Was there nothing better to occupy the mind in retirement than that?

There was a programme on the television more recently about the assassination of Anwar Sadat, the President of Egypt, that jogged my memory of another holiday that Margarita and I spent without the girls, whom we had left behind in Madrid. We had toured Italy, before flying back via Barcelona, staying one or two nights in the second City of Spain. Rome, Venice, Florence, Pisa, Genoa and Milan were the chief ports of call that year.

Eight thousand Italian lire sounded a large sum to us at the time. But the receptionist at the Venice hotel where we were checking in, assured us that this was a perfectly fair price to pay a porter, for carrying our bags a very short distance from the ferry. We paid the amount grudgingly, without translating the amount into a more familiar currency, but when we later did our mathematics, we decided it was a hefty bill for such a mean task. After that, we compared everything we spent, to the amount earned by that porter; may God bless him! Nothing seemed so expensive thereafter; the ride on the gondola being the most touristy and costly among the touristy activities we ventured into. We ambled around the spectacular squares and admired the canals from the bridges and walkways. I took many photographs, from which I attempted several water colour paintings. But I often wonder if our great-grandchildren will ever be able to see Venice as a living city, threatened as it is by global warming and the lack of a solid foundation. The truth is, Venice is slowly sinking, and there is no guarantee that the fight against the decay of its historic buildings is going to succeed. Add to this, the predicted global rise in the sea level, and the future of Venice looks bleak.

No tourist visit to Italy would be complete without seeing the Leaning Tower of Pisa. The architect, who was responsible for the faulty foundations of the tower, could never have known how much money was going to be made out of his error! The aim now is to ensure that the tower does not lean so far as to risk its complete collapse. An expert recently assured us that it would actually be many hundreds of years before there was any danger of that.

Florence is arguably one of the most beautiful cities in the world; its wealth of splendid architecture, nestled in a valley in one of the softest and dreamiest parts of the Old World. It is hardly big enough to warrant the title 'City', but the authorities have done well to keep its charm. And the pizza was good too! We should have spent more time there.

We have visited Rome twice. What a contrast to Florence! Rome is a mad City of honking taxis and expensive restaurants on the one hand, and incredible Roman ruins on the other. We did the tourist things, but avoided getting ripped off by the taxi drivers, who have a reputation for taking you around in circles to earn a few extra lire! We were warned to watch our bags and pockets. We succeeded in avoiding the loss of possessions too.

It was from Milan that we flew back to Spain, and it was in Barcelona that we heard the news of Sadat's assassination. Perhaps it was because Barcelona was 'home' to us, but we loved it. It was so full of life! I remember questioning the absence of street cafes in Nairobi, a phenomenon that is so Mediterranean. If only Nairobi had them! And why not? The climate is hospitable enough. Sure enough, tables and chairs have started to creep out of Nairobi doorways of late.

Indonesia was one destination made possible with the Coca-Cola's policy of allowing expatriate staff to use their airfare entitlement as they wished. Andy Sloan had been transferred by BAT to Jakarta and he invited us to stay with them. By this time, both our girls were away in Europe. In April 1986, we booked a round trip; Nairobi to Jakarta, to Jogjakarta on the south coast of the Island of Java, to Bali, to Bangkok, the capital of Thailand, and back to Nairobi. Due to a mistake by the travel agent, we were booked to fly to Balikpapan, an oil port on the southern coast of Borneo, part of Indonesia. Apparently, there is nothing there but a smelly oil refinery, surrounded by tropical jungle. I picked up the mistake through my interest in looking at a map to see where we were going. How mad we would have been to spend four days, either as guests of Shell, or camping among the cannibals of the Borneo rain forest!

Jakarta was fun as guests of the Sloans. Their friendly house girl was happy to babysit for little two-year-old Chris, while we dined out in their favourite eating places. There was plenty of laughter, even without smoking the weed! Andy's smile and broad grin was highly infectious, so a few puffs were superfluous. It was as well, because in Indonesia, heavy jail sentences are meted out to those caught with drugs, however much we might have argued that marijuana was harmless.

After a brief stay, we flew the short distance across Java to the city of Jogjakarta, home to a million people. The main memories are a visit to a fabulous Buddhist temple and a lunch of frogs' legs. We had never tried them before. Later, we came to learn how the people ill-treat the poor creatures in the process of removing the legs. Had we known at the time, perhaps we would not have deigned to sample them. Next on the itinerary was Bali, that romantic little island next to Java. We were unimpressed by Bali's main holiday resort on the south coast, having come from Kenya. But the surfing looked impressive, and if you were in the mood for a beach massage, there was plenty of opportunity. It was only after crossing to the northern side of the island that we came to realise that the beach we had left was the only sandy one to be found on the island.

Interestingly, Bali is Hindu, whereas Islam is the religion of the rest of Indonesia. One evening, we watched a play of the Ramayana, performed especially for tourists. During a walk, we came across a colourful funeral procession. The 'mourners' were visibly and surprisingly happy and wanted to include us in their ceremony. The body, bedecked with flowers, showed us a peaceful face. Neither we nor the family was embarrassed by our presence.

Bali's interior is mountainous. Our minibus took us on a winding road over the mountains to the north coast. It was interesting to see how unfriendly, almost aggressive, were the highland people, in contrast to those we met on our arrival. We stayed in a family-run hotel, the owners of which treated us like their own kin. It was just as well because there was no beach, so that swimming was out of the question.

From Bali we flew to Bangkok via Jakarta. We had kept in touch with Jay

Smith, the Kodak man who had played a part in my securing the job with Coca-Cola. He and his family lived in a big house with a swimming pool. If you are thinking of visiting Bangkok in April, take my advice; forget it! No amount of dipping in the tepid water of the pool will bring relief to the sweating body. Fortunately, the bedrooms were air conditioned, but a trip to the toilet in the night was rather like walking through a steam bath. Neither was fighting the traffic jams of Bangkok any more comfortable. But we had to do a bit of sightseeing; after all, we may never get to see Bangkok again! So, we took a tour, which included a visit to the Golden Temple, (if that is the proper name), some splendid gardens, and a boat trip along some of the canals of the City. These canals are lined with wooden houses, from which small children frolicked in the murky water. They also provide alternative routes, avoiding the congestion of the roadways, (Photo No. 82). The Golden Temple was magnificent. It obviously took a great deal to impress Christopher, because, when asked what he thought of the temple, he said in a very uninterested voice that it was okay, or some similar expression. In Photo No. 83, we are seen dining in a Bangkok restaurant. We were to receive Christmas cards from the Smiths for a few years thereafter, always portraying a smiling family group, typically American. Finally, we lost touch with them. Relationships are like plants; they need feeding and watering, otherwise they wither away.

The last overseas holiday of the decade was the skiing expedition our family of five made to the Pyrenees. It was also the year that Margarita's father passed away. Isabel was studying Spanish in Madrid, and Cathy was staying with her temporarily. We did a bit of shopping for warm clothes in Madrid. I still have the thick sweater and double-sided belt that I bought that Easter of 1989, thirty-five years ago!

We hired a car in Madrid and headed for the mountains, hoping that the warm April sun had not reduced the ski slopes to a mushy grey. We passed Lerida, and then up into the southern slopes of the Pyrenees. To our relief, we found the snow, although it was beginning to melt on the lower slopes. We stayed in a *pension* in the village nearest the slopes. It was cold at night, but the sun shone faithfully each day.

It was my second attempt with skis, the first being the Christmas I had spent with Ian van Rijn at his parents' house in Switzerland. For the rest of the family it was the first. We laughed! Margarita sat on her bottom in the snow for much of the time. Christopher was only five years old and needed help, something his mother could not give him from her sitting position, due to constant laughter! Isabel suffered from an abnormality in her knees. Her kneecaps were too small and kept coming out of their sockets. She was therefore nervous of going too far, or too fast, and stuck to the lower slopes. Only Cathy and I made full use of the slopes. Despite my weak left knee, I had little difficulty in taking up the correct posture. It was great fun.

After a few days skiing, we drove westwards to Galicia, to stay a while with Margarita's ailing father. It was to be the last time the children and I saw him. The photograph of him, standing in his raincoat with his walking stick with Cathy and Christopher is lost, but in Photo No. 84, he is with his wife, Lolita. In Photo No. 85, Christopher receives a hug from his *Abuelito*. Soon after this, his best friend passed away and he lost the will to live. Margarita flew back to Spain only two months after our Easter visit, when her father had been admitted to ICU. She told us later that it was distressing to see him tied down to the bed, lest he should pull away the tubes that were keeping him alive. He pleaded with his daughter to remove them, but how could she, when his own wife was there! Did she not have more authority than the daughter? Margarita was angry with Lolita for not allowing him to die peacefully. But Lolita and the doctors would not listen to her. She was overwhelmed with sorrow when her father told her to go, if she couldn't remove the lifelines! How sad!

Having described some of the memorable holidays spent overseas in the 1980's, let me take you back home to Kenya; to New Muthaiga where we lived, and to Coca-Cola, where I worked the best part of my waking hours.

The Coca-Cola Company is a leading multinational. In the 1980's, under the dynamic leadership of the Cuban Wizkid, Roberto Goizuetta, the Company was striving, and succeeding in keeping ahead of the pack. The Company paid its senior management staff handsomely but intended to exact their 'pound of flesh'. The pressure on us to contribute to the increase in shareholder value was considerable. A conference of Finance Managers took place in a hotel on the West Coast of Florida in 1986, aimed at encouraging us to think 'outside the box.' I think it was the time when I began to suffer from acute stress.

I joined the elite on the 11th floor of Bruce House. I was granted a larger office, was given my own secretary and a qualified assistant accountant. Deadlines were tightened, and returns to Head Office became more onerous. Added to that, my 'protector,' Eddie Ferrari, took retirement, and his place was taken by an aggressive Egyptian, Rafik Ayub, whose character suited the new aggressive approach that Coca-Cola had deemed necessary. Life under Rafik Ayub was not so easy. It was not that he was unfair or unkind but the pressure on him to perform rolled onto his managers, and I began to see my weaknesses and limitations.

I remember well the time I had to fly to England to attend an East Africa Region meeting at the Division Office in Windsor. My job was to present the results for the just concluded year, and explain the difference between the actual and budgeted figures. I knew that interpreting figures was not my strong point. Neither was standing in front of Coca-Cola's senior managers! I awoke in my hotel room very early in the morning of the presentation, terrified of the trauma to come. As it happened, I discharged my duty, rather nervously, but I could only relax when it was over. Windsor is a quaint little English town, dominated by the huge castle, home to royalty for hundreds of years. I remember walking through the town with Alan Jackson, who was the Division Finance Manager at that time, and my immediate financial superior. He was a gentle man in his early sixties. His favourite shop was Thornton's, the makers of sumptuous and extremely expensive chocolates. Alan loved chocolates and his teeth were testimony to this. He also said that exercise was a complete waste of time. It was no surprise that, despite his agile mind, he went around in a rapidly ageing body. In fact, he was a candidate for heart disease. I never heard anything of him after leaving Coca-Cola in 1990. At that time, he was about two years from retirement.

The Coca-Cola Company acquired Columbia Pictures during my time. Perhaps the Board thought that some advertising could be done by way of the screen. Columbia Pictures decided to make a film in Kenya, and it was to be financed from the substantial liquid resources of the Company that were stuck in the country. As the Finance Manager, I had been depositing surplus funds with banks at the most favourable interest rates. Now, the money was to finance the film, which was called 'Sheena, Queen of the Jungle'. I paid out over one-hundred-million Kenya shillings over the period of the shooting. We did get to see the film later. I think it was a complete failure. The mules they painted in black and white stripes to resemble zebras were totally unrealistic! As for the actors and actresses, Well!

Having lived in the big house in New Muthaiga since 1981, we began to tire of the life. There were several factors that contributed to the decision to move from there into a smaller house in 1990. Firstly, our house servant, who had been with us for many years, began to play up. We have since come to see this as a common phenomenon, especially with Luhyas. He had never wanted to move from the convenience of Westlands, while his nose had been put out of joint by the arrival of Tracy, whose personality was strong enough to resist domination by the male. When small annoyances failed, such as spoiling my paints and our audio cassettes, or deliberately cutting the straps of sandals, Jackson resorted to more serious actions. We were convinced that he was behind a spate of break-ins and attempted robberies. Thieves entered the ground floor study one night and stole the stereo system. Another time, they broke into the kitchen and went off with, among other things, a case of wine, but could not force the strong, locked door into the rest of the house. I was awoken another night by a noise downstairs. I went to investigate. I pulled aside the curtain in the dining room, and there, on the other side of the glass, was a black face peering in at me. He ran away, after hurling a stone at the window, breaking one pane. We were quite sure Jackson was behind those goings on, with or without the connivance of the night watchman. Tracy later confirmed to us that she had actually seen Jackson at the window of his room at the time the robbers were attempting an entry through a window.

There was another, potentially serious situation. A young *Mkamba,* whom we had taken on as a gardener, was playing with our little five-year-old son. Christopher was able to tell someone about it. We did not want to go through the business of sacking the man, when we were considering a move anyway. The robberies, the energy and expense of upkeeping a large house and garden, then the gardener's antics, decided it for us. We had lent Jackson money to buy a *shamba* and had paid for him to take driving lessons. Now he was becoming cocky. We got to hear that he was planning to take home a bed that we had bought, and which we had made clear to him was not his property. Margarita warned him against taking it, but he did anyway. We dismissed him, which I believe is what he wanted. He could now drive, and must have thought that he would get a job as a driver, which would be better paid than being a house servant. And his loan balance was still over Shs.10,000/-, a small part of which we were able to recover from his final dues. So, we parted ways. But it was not the last we saw of him. He secured a job as a driver with a diplomat. I have no doubt the job was better paid than the one he had with us. The son of his employer studied at Kenton College with Christopher, and we would sometimes meet Jackson at the school. By the way he greeted us, one would think we were the best of friends. I have heard similar stories elsewhere. I can only conclude that the kind of behaviour he had displayed is acceptable in the eyes of his race.

Jeff Austen-Brown was the director who had employed me at Westlands Motors back in 1973. When we decided to find a new home late in 1989, I rang him and asked him to reserve a flat in Norfolk Towers, a block of apartments near the Norfolk Hotel and a short walk from the centre of town. Then we found a flat there under strange circumstances. I am tempted to believe that there are no coincidences, and this was one of those cases that others may claim to be coincidental. We had already been often to Norfolk Towers to visit the Spences. Anne had been kind to us at the time Margarita was hospitalised, ten days after Christopher was born. The day we decided to take another look at the flats, we passed by Block B, on the way to the swimming pool. We were surprised to find a family we knew, sitting on their patio of B43, a ground floor flat. Having greeted one another, we told them the reason for our visit that day. Surprise, surprise! They told us they were about to vacate the flat that very month. It was perfect for us. An anxious call to Jeff, thinking that perhaps it had already been taken, and, relieved to find that it was still available, the deal was done. The rent of Shs.27,500/- was within the Company's limit. We moved in before Christmas 1989.

No. 74

No. 75

No. 76

No. 77

No. 78

No. 79

No. 80

No. 81

No. 82

No. 83

No. 84

No. 85

No. 86

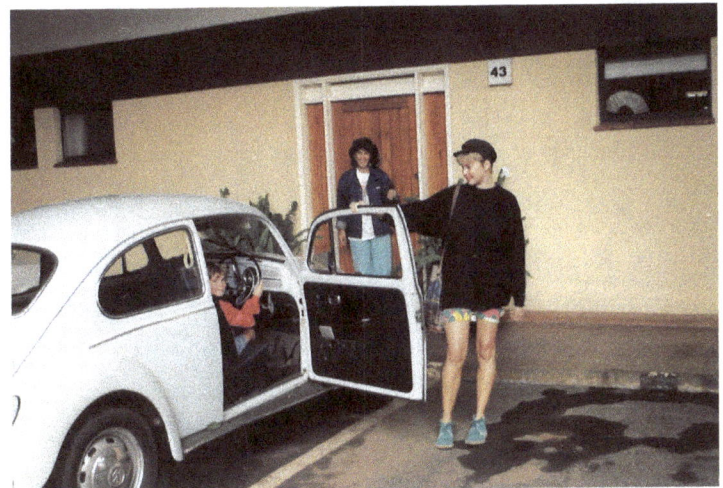

No. 87

No. 88

No. 89

No. 90

No. 91

No. 92

No. 93

No. 94

A stroll across the grass and we had a private swimming pool. Very few tenants used it and we did not have the responsibility of maintaining it. We swam almost every morning. In fine weather, we ate on the patio, and the lawn in front of the flat was a playground for Christopher. At first, he objected to the move from New Muthaiga, but after some time he settled down. Margarita and I never missed the old house. Reuben King'oo, who had been working for a family near our Muthaiga house, and was well known to us, came to work for us, commuting daily from Kibera, as there were no quarters provided by Norfolk Towers. As I write, Reuben is working full time for me in Lamu, thirty-four years later!

I took to walking to work, along Harry Thuku Road and down Muindi Mbingu Street to Bruce House. The only disadvantage of living in town was the higher level of air pollution. New Muthaiga, being well out of the City-centre and at a higher altitude, was a healthier place to be. Flat B43, Norfolk Towers was our home until April 1998, when the management increased the rent to a level above our acceptability. And a very happy home it was! In

Photo No. 86, Christopher is with Mum and Dad during one of their visits to Kenya.

The year 1990 was a watershed in my life. It was the year that I left Coca-Cola, and shortly thereafter came the end of my professional career. It happened this way. Around March of that year, the stress of my job began to impact my mental health to a point where I was unable to think clearly. I became confused. When I broke down in tears one day, Margarita decided enough was enough. She went to the office and told Charles Mukora, since Rafik Ayoub was out of the country, that I was not fit to go to work, and if I didn't take a break, there was a risk of my having a nervous breakdown. Charles Mukora was sympathetic and gave me two weeks special leave. Margarita saw me off to England to stay with my Mum, arguing that at times such as those, going back to one's roots was the best cure. So, I cleared Coca-Cola from my mind for two weeks. It was the best thing I could have done. I returned to Nairobi refreshed. However, it was clear that I needed to make some drastic changes to my life. Back in the office, I went to discuss my future with Rafik. I had missed a couple of deadlines for submission of monthly management accounts to Atlanta; one of the main issues that the internal auditors had highlighted in their report. My financial bosses took these lapses very seriously, and so it was mutually agreed that I should resign as the East Africa Region Finance Manager. It was June 1990, I was forty-eight, and had worked for the company for almost nine years, but well short of the number of years required to earn a pension. But the Company was unexpectedly generous. They agreed to pay me in full up to the end of 1990, subject to returning the company car and cashing in the Coca-Cola shares that I had been awarded over the years. But Coca-Cola shares had increased tremendously in value, and the proceeds of sale amounted to over US$90,000. It was with relief that I parted company with Coca-Cola.

I gave up the company car. I had bought a white Toyota Carina, KQR 810, from my previous employer, Westlands Motors. It was a very reliable vehicle and I was fond of it. It was now the family's only car. But not for long! One day, around September 1990, it was stolen from outside The Sarit Centre, where we had gone shopping for only a short time. I had parked in the street a few yards from the main entrance. When we emerged from the shopping centre, I was puzzled. I was sure that I knew where I had parked it. But it was not there. Surveying the entire length of the street without success, we came to the sad realisation that our lovely white Toyota Carina had been stolen. It was insured for theft, but could the money from the insurance company compensate for the loss? We duly reported it to the Parklands police station, and the officer who took the details was confident of recovery. But it was not to be. We never saw that car again. At the time of reporting it stolen, it was probably safely in a workshop somewhere in the outskirts of the City, undergoing a major facelift, new number plates and a complete respray. Or perhaps it was already being dismantled for spare parts, to be sold in one of the hundreds of spare parts shops. But that is not the most amazing part of the story. I had to find a new car. That led me, on the following Sunday morning, to visit the weekly car sale in Westlands. Walking up and down the streets around The Sarit Centre, I found a 1969 turquoise Volkswagen Beetle in excellent condition. I had always liked the hands-on feel of that car. It was the model that had taken us down the Garden Route from Durban to Cape Town in 1975. Standing beside the car was an Englishman I had met before. He had worked at the Norfolk Hotel, but had ventured into tourism on his own. He wanted Shs.60,000/- for it. I thought it was a very fair price. I went for a spin, and ended up buying it. Margarita was very negative when I spilt the beans, but she soon overcame her fear of never being able to drive it. It served us well for many years. In Photo No. 87, Christopher is at the wheel outside our Norfolk Towers flat. But its history from that day to this is another tale. The incredible part of the story is that the VW had been parked in *exactly* the same spot from which the Carina had been stolen the week before!

On the 13th July 1990, we had joined in the celebrations for my parents' golden wedding anniversary. In Photo No. 88, Mum and Dad relax in the garden of Watersmeet. A large number of Mum's extended family were there to join in the celebrations. In Photo No. 89, almost all of Mum's siblings are present, with spouses. This was without doubt the last occasion when they were all together. Of that generation of Walkers, only Eileen remains with us. As I write, she is well on the way to her 104th birthday! Several other photos of that special day are included here. Photo No. 90 shows seven-year-old Christopher with his doting grandparents. Cousins whom I would rarely meet are captured, in Photo No. 91; Anne and husband, Mike, and in Photo No. 92; Marion and husband, Bob. John was visiting that summer. In Photo No. 93, he stands with me, and our sister, Jean. He can also be seen in Photo No. 94, with his Auntie Eileen and Uncle Doug.

Having left Coca-Cola, and with no clear idea of where my future would lead me, I registered a business as a financial consultant, and was given a work permit. For some months, I did part-time work, mainly for my ex-employer, as well as producing a monthly economic report for the Kenyan distributor for Mitsubishi vehicles for a paltry sum of Shs.3,000/-. But consultancy work was not for me. I was to make a fundamental change in my life at the beginning of 1991.

EPILOGUE

ONE OF THE POPULAR SUBJECTS for debate is that concerning whether our lives are pre-programmed or not. Do we choose the parents to whom we are born? Or does the Almighty decide, and dictate every twist and turn of our lives? Or does every moment of our lives offer the chance of a different experience? Do the choices we make hundreds of times a day contribute to the paths we take?

When I look back at past years, I see myriad moments when the future could have turned the corner and taken an entirely different path. I choose but a few examples. In 1954, my parents were on the point of emigrating to Canada. A chance to work in Kuwait for a shorter time changed all that. Then, had I taken a different career on leaving school, my life would have taken a different course. Then, had I passed that junction while scooting through Berwick-upon-Tweed a few seconds earlier or a few seconds later, I would have avoided the collision with the van. Then, there were thousands of moments in which Margarita's early life could have stepped aside from the path it finally took, and which permitted that 'chance meeting' at the table in the dining room of No. 2, Church Crescent. Then, had we bought that alluring house with the orchard outside Bath, perhaps we would have stayed there, rather than move to Whitchurch. Then, in 1970, when Cooper Brothers was unable to secure a work permit for The West Indies, we opted instead for Africa, a Continent we had never considered. Then, when the Finance Director of Mercat persuaded me to attend the interview in London for the job in Nairobi, we decided to give it a go, having previously chosen to remain in England. Lastly, had my father not survived the sinking of his wartime ship in 1940, I would not have come into the World in the same physical form at all! All these, and millions of other moments, could have changed the course of our history. I cannot dare to imagine having missed those wonderful seventeen years in Kenya, this land of opportunity, but, a different route into the future could have given us an equally exciting and satisfying thirty years: who knows? Was every event in my life and in the lives of my family predestined? I would love to know!

THE END

www.ingramcontent.com/pod-product-compliance
Lightning Source LLC
Chambersburg PA
CBHW071157160426
43196CB00011B/2111